CW00455143

The Scent of Flowers at Night

Also by Leïla Slimani
and available in English:

Lullaby
Adèle
Sex and Lies
The Country of Others

Leïla Slimani

The Scent of
Flowers at Night

Translated from the French by Sam Taylor

CORONET

First published in Great Britain in 2023 by Coronet
An imprint of Hodder & Stoughton
An Hachette UK company

1

Copyright © Éditions Stock 2021
English translation copyright © Sam Taylor 2023

The right of Leïla Slimani to be identified as the Author
of the Work has been asserted by her in accordance with
the Copyright, Designs and Patents Act 1988.

A CIP catalogue record for this title is available from the British Library

Hardback ISBN 9781529399653
eBook ISBN 9781529399646

Typeset in Bembo by Hewer Text UK Ltd, Edinburgh
Printed and bound in Great Britain by Clays Ltd, Elcograf S.p.A.

Hodder & Stoughton policy is to use papers that are natural, renewable
and recyclable products and made from wood grown in sustainable
forests. The logging and manufacturing processes are expected to
conform to the environmental regulations of the country of origin.

Hodder & Stoughton Ltd
Carmelite House
50 Victoria Embankment
London EC4Y 0DZ

www.hodder.co.uk

'If solitude exists, and I don't know if it does, one should certainly have the right to dream of it occasionally as a paradise.'

Albert Camus

'Where there is art and genius, there can never be such things as old age or loneliness or sickness, and death itself is half.'

Anton Chekhov

To Jean-Marie Laclavetine,
who helped me become a writer

To my friend Salman Rushdie

Paris, December 2018

The first rule when you are trying to write a novel is to say no. No, I won't meet up for a drink. No, I can't look after my sick nephew. No, I'm not free for lunch, for an interview. No, I can't go for a walk or see a film. You have to say no so often that the offers become rarer, the telephone stops ringing, and you start to regret the fact that all your emails are adverts. You have to say no so often that people think you're an arrogant misanthrope, a pathological loner. You have to build a fortress of refusal around yourself so that all those requests and invitations will smash against its walls. This is what my editor told me when I began writing novels. It's what I read in all the essays on writing – by Roth, by Stevenson, and by Hemingway, who boiled the advice down into a simple dictum: 'The telephone and visitors are the work destroyers.' He added that, once the writer has acquired the necessary discipline, once literature has become the centre, the sole horizon of their life, solitude becomes easy. 'The further you go in writing, the more alone you are. Most of your best and oldest friends die. Others move away. [. . .] You are more alone because that is how you must work and the time to work is shorter all the time and if you waste it you feel you have committed a sin for which there is no forgiveness.'

For the last few months, I have forced myself to follow this advice. To put in place the conditions of my isolation. In the morning, as soon as my children are at school, I go up to my office, and I don't come out again until evening. I turn off my phone. I sit at my desk or I lie on the sofa. I always end up feeling cold, and as the hours pass, I put on a sweater, then another one, before finally wrapping myself in a blanket.

My office measures ten by twelve feet. A window on the right-hand wall overlooks a courtyard. The air there is filled with restaurant smells: detergent and lentils with bacon. In front of me, a long, wooden plank serves as my desk. The shelves are cluttered with history books and newspaper cuttings. On the left-hand wall are Post-it notes in various colours. Each colour corresponds to a particular year: pink for 1953, yellow for 1954, green for 1955. On these squares of paper, I have written names of characters, ideas for scenes. Mathilde at the cinema. Aicha in the quince orchard. One day when I was feeling inspired, I set down the chronology for this novel on which I am working and which does not yet have a title.* It tells the story of a family in the small town of Meknès between the end of the Second World War and the beginning of Moroccan independence. A map of the town, printed in 1952, is spread out on the floor. You can clearly see the borders between the Arab quarters, the Jewish mellah and the European district.

Today is not a good day. I've been sitting on this chair for hours, and my characters aren't speaking

* Translator's note: This is the book that became *The Country of Others* (2020).

to me. Nothing comes. Not a word, not an image, not the hint of a musical phrase that might lead me to put a few sentences down on the page. All day long, I've smoked too much, I've wasted my time in rabbit holes online, I've taken a nap. Still nothing has come. I wrote a chapter, which I then deleted. Now I think about a story a friend told me. I don't know if it's true, but I liked it a lot. While he was working on *Anna Karenina*, Tolstoy suffered a severe case of writer's block. For weeks, he didn't write a single line. His editor, who had paid him a considerable advance for the book, was alarmed by the delay in receiving the manuscript and, after writing several letters and getting no response, decided to take the train to Tolstoy's house to question him. When he arrived at Yasnaya Polyana, the novelist welcomed him into his home. The editor asked what was happening with the novel, and Tolstoy replied: 'Anna Karenina has left. I am waiting for her to return.'

Of course, I cannot compare myself to that Russian genius, or any of my novels to his masterpieces. But I am obsessed by that phrase: 'Anna Karenina has left'. I, too, sometimes feel as if my characters have escaped me, that they have gone away to lead another life and will return only when they are ready. They are utterly indifferent to my distress, my prayers; indifferent even to the love that I feel for them. They have left, and I must wait for them to return. When they are here, the days fly by. I mutter to myself; I write as fast as I can, always afraid that my hands will not be able to keep up with the speed of my thoughts. In such moments, I am terrified by the idea that something might break my concentration, like a tightrope walker who makes the momentary mistake of looking down. When my characters are here, my whole life revolves around that obsession, and the outside world ceases to exist. It becomes nothing more than a film set through which I walk, my mind lit up, at the end of a long, sweet day of work. I live apart from others. This seclusion seems to me the one condition necessary for Life to happen. As if, by separating myself from the noise of the world, by protecting myself, another world might emerge from within me. A 'once upon a time'. I slip into this small, silent space, far from the madding crowd, and sink beneath the thick foam of things. I do not close myself to the world; on the contrary, I experience it more strongly than ever.

Writing is discipline. It is giving up on happiness, on the little joys of everyday life. You can't try to cure or console yourself. In fact, you must cultivate your sorrows the way lab techs cultivate bacteria in glass jars. You must reopen old wounds, stir up old memories, relive old shames, retaste old tears. To write, you must refuse yourself to others; refuse them your presence, your love. You must disappoint your friends and your children. For me, this discipline is a source of satisfaction, even happiness, and at the same time, the cause of my melancholy. My whole life is dictated by these imperatives. I must be silent. I must concentrate. I must stay seated. I must resist my desires. Writing is a sort of imprisonment, but its very shackles contain within them the possibility of an immense, dizzying freedom. I remember the moment when I first became aware of this. It was in December 2013, and I was writing my first novel, *Adèle*. At the time, I was living in an apartment on Boulevard Rochechouart. I had a little boy, and I could only write when he was at nursery. I was sitting at the dining room table and I thought: *Right now, you can say absolutely anything you want. You – the polite child who was taught always to behave, to rein yourself in – you can tell the truth. You don't have to consider anyone else's feelings. You have nothing to fear. Write whatever you want.* In that vast place of freedom, the social mask falls from your face. You can be someone else. You are no longer defined by your gender, your social class, your religion or your nationality. Writing is discovering the freedom to invent yourself and the world.

Of course, there are many hard days like this one, and sometimes they pile up, one after another. It can be deeply discouraging. But writing is as addictive as opium. And the writer, like all addicts, forgets the sickening side effects, the withdrawal symptoms, the loneliness, and remembers only the ecstasy. The writer will do anything to feel that high again, that sublime moment when their characters start speaking through them, when life pulsates with possibility.

It's five o'clock. Outside, night has fallen. I haven't turned on the desk lamp, so my office is in darkness too. I start to believe that in this darkness, something might happen, a last-minute flash of inspiration. Sometimes, in the absence of light, dreams and hallucinations grow wild like vines. I open my laptop and reread a scene I wrote yesterday. It's about an afternoon that my character spends at the cinema. What films were they showing at the Empire cinema in Meknès in 1953? I do some research. I find some very moving old photographs online, and quickly send them to my mother. I start to write. I remember what my grandmother told me once, about the big, heavy-handed Moroccan usherette who used to grab cigarettes out of people's mouths if they smoked during the film. I am getting ready to begin a new chapter when an alarm buzzes on my phone. I have a meeting in half an hour. A meeting I didn't manage to say no to. Alina, the editor I am about to meet, is a persuasive woman. A passionate woman, who has a proposal for me. I think about sending her a message: some simple lie to get me out of this meeting. I could make up an excuse involving my children, tell her that I'm ill, that I missed my train, that my mother needs me. But I don't do any of these things. Instead, I put on my coat, slip the laptop into my bag, leave my lair, and venture out into the world.

In the metro, on the way to the meeting, I curse myself. 'You'll never get anywhere if you can't focus fully on your work.' Outside the café, where I smoke a cigarette as I wait for Alina, I swear to myself that I will say no. Say no to anything she suggests, no matter how interesting it might sound. Say: 'I'm writing a novel, and I don't want to do anything else. Maybe later, but not now.' I have to project an aura of inflexibility, an unbreakable determination.

We sit on the terrace despite the December cold. In Paris, nobody seems to find it odd when people sit outside for a drink in the middle of winter, holding a cigarette between their frozen fingers. I order a glass of wine, thinking it might dissolve my melancholy. My ridiculous melancholy. How can anyone be sad just because they haven't managed to write?

Alina talks to me about her project, a new series of books entitled 'My Night at the Museum'. But I am so riddled with doubt and guilt that I hardly hear a word she says. By the time my glass is empty, I am starting to think that I may never be able to write again, that I will never finish another novel. I am so anguished that it hurts to swallow.

'So, what do you think,' Alina asks me, 'about the idea of being locked up for a night in a museum?'

It wasn't the museum that convinced me. Alina's proposal was tempting, of course: sleeping in the Punta della Dogana, the legendary Venice monument now transformed into a museum of contemporary art. In truth, the thought of sleeping close to works of art leaves me cold. I nurture no fantasies about having those paintings and sculptures all to myself. I don't believe I will see them any better without the crowds, that I will gain a deeper understanding of their meaning because we are face to face. Not for one moment did I think I might have something significant to write about contemporary art. I don't know much about it.

I'm not really interested in it. No, what I liked about Alina's proposal, what drove me to say yes, was the idea of being locked up. The idea that nobody could get hold of me, that the world would be out of reach. Being alone in a place that nobody else could enter, a place from which I couldn't escape: it's a writer's fantasy. All of us have these cloistered dreams, visions of a room of our own where we would be both prisoner and guard. I've found it in all the private diaries, all the letters written by novelists: that desire for silence, that dream of an isolation where there is nothing to prevent the act of creation. The history of literature is filled with famous recluses, intensely solitary men and women. It has been built over years – from Hölderlin to Emily Brontë, from Petrarch to Flaubert, from Kafka to Rilke – this myth of the writer isolated from the world, separated from the crowd, determined to devote their life to literature.

A friend of mine, a very successful writer, admitted to me once that he had never been as happy as he was the day when, on the verge of exhaustion, he broke his leg. 'I spent a month and a half locked in my apartment, and I wrote. And nobody could say a thing, because I had the perfect excuse of being in a plaster cast from my foot to my hip.' I have often thought of picking up a hammer and breaking my own tibia. Writing is a battle for immobility, for concentration. A physical combat in which you must constantly master your desire to live, your desire to be happy.

I would like to withdraw from the world. To enter my novel the way a nun enters a convent. To make a vow of silence, of modesty, of total submission to my work. I would like to be devoted solely to words, to forget every aspect of ordinary life, not to have to worry about anything beyond the fates of my characters. For my previous novels, I did withdraw in that way – to a house in the countryside or a hotel in a foreign city. For three or four days, I would be locked away and I would lose all sense of time. To finish *Lullaby*, I went to Normandy on my own. For a whole week, I saw no one. I didn't hear the sound of my own voice. I didn't wash, didn't brush my hair. I hung around the silent house in pyjamas, eating whatever I wanted whenever I felt hungry. I didn't answer the phone, didn't open any letters or bills; I shirked all my obligations. I would wake in the middle of the night and furiously begin writing down an idea that had come to me in a dream. My room was in chaos, my bed covered with books, papers and half-eaten brioches. The latter probably explains why, one night, I woke with a start: my laptop was open beside me, and when I turned on the light, I saw that my arms, my books, my sheets, were swarming with ants, all of them running frantically in circles, as in some nightmarish dance. Rarely in my life have I felt so happy.

That evening, as I get home, I am already regretting my decision. As if being locked up for one night is going to rid me of my writer's block. In my library, I look up anything I can find on Venice in general, and the city's Sea Customs House, in which the museum is located, in particular. I own several guides, although all I have ever used them for is finding cheap restaurants and working out how to use the *vaporetto*.

I pull a copy of Paul Morand's *Venises* from a shelf. Opening it randomly, I come upon this passage: 'I would escape. To what, I didn't know, but I sensed that the direction of my life would be turned outward, elsewhere, towards the light. [. . .] At the same time, there began that swing of the pendulum that never left me, a desire – probably prenatal – for a narrowing, the pleasure of living in a small room, vexed by the intoxication of the desert, the sea, the steppes. I hated fences, doors; borders and walls offended me.' I have always experienced life in the same way. In that wavering between the lure of outside and the safety of inside; between the desire to know, to be known, and the temptation to retreat completely within my inner existence. I have always been torn between the wish to stay in my room and the constant craving for diversion, company, the chance to forget myself. I want simultaneously to be disciplined, to remain calm, and to tear myself free from my current condition, my origin, attaining liberty through movement. I live in that endless tension: fear of others and desire for others, austerity and festivity, shadow and light, humility and ambition.

Sometimes I think that if I didn't talk to anyone, if I kept all my thoughts to myself, they wouldn't seem so banal when I shared them with others. Conversation is the writer's worst enemy. I should say nothing, take refuge in a deep and lasting silence. If I forced myself to embrace mutism, I could cultivate metaphors and flights of lyricism the way gardeners grow flowers in greenhouses. If

I became a hermit, I would see the things that life in society prevents me from seeing. I would hear the sounds buried by the voices of others and the hum of everyday existence. When you live in the world, it seems to me, your secrets go stale, your inner treasures lose their lustre; you damage something that, if kept secret, might have given you the substance of a novel. The outside world acts upon our thoughts like air on the frescos in that ancient villa that Fellini filmed in *Roma*, vanishing as soon as they are discovered. As if too much attention, too much light, can destroy our inner night.

'I have set up my standard as an invalid and no one bothers me,' Virginia Woolf wrote in her diary. 'No one asks me to do anything. Vainly, I have the feeling that this is of my choice, not theirs; and there is a luxury in being quiet in the heart of chaos. Directly I talk and exert my wits in talk I get a dull damp rather headachy day.' Revealing yourself, mixing with others, sometimes causes this strange sense of shame and debasement. When you write, chit-chat can feel like an attack; conversation can become unbearable. Maybe because it contains everything you fear: clichés, platitudes, all those ready-made phrases that people use without thinking. Sayings and set expressions can be dangerous in those moments when a writer is attempting to capture something ambiguous, hazy, uncertain.

When my father found himself at the centre of a political and financial scandal, I suffered terribly from such figures of speech. Trite remarks are like little daggers stabbed into life's wounds. People say: 'There's no smoke without fire.' But there are fires that burn for a long time without any smoke escaping from the building. There are flames that bloom in secret. And then there is the kind of black, sticky smoke that sullies everything, choking hearts, driving away friends and happiness. You can spend years searching for the fire that caused this smoke. And sometimes you will never find it.

What isn't said belongs to you forever. Writing is a way of playing with silence, of slyly revealing unspeakable secrets in real life. Literature is an art of withholding. You hold yourself back as you do in the first days of love when banal phrases pop into your head, passionate declarations that you force yourself not to say so as not to damage the beauty of the moment. Literature is made up of an erotica of silence. What matters is what is left unsaid. In truth, it is perhaps the age in which we live and not only my work as a writer that drives me to seek out solitude and peace. I wonder what Stefan Zweig would have thought of this society obsessed by the display of self, by the dramatisation of existence. What would he have said about this age, when the expression of any point of view can expose you to violence and hate, when the artist has to fall in with public opinion? When you write two hundred and eighty characters on a momentary urge? In *The World of Yesterday*, he penned an admiring portrait of the poet Rainer Maria Rilke. He wondered what the future would hold for writers of that kind, those for whom literature was an existential vocation. He wrote: 'But is not ours a time which does not grant, even to the purest and the most secluded, any quiet for waiting and ripening and contemplation and collecting one's self?'

Venice, April 2019

If I had nothing to say about contemporary art, what was I going to be able to say about Venice? There is nothing more frightening for a writer than those subjects about which it seems that everything has already been written. ('Avoid those forms that are too facile and ordinary: they are the hardest to work with, and it takes great, fully ripened power to create something individual where good, even glorious, traditions exist in abundance,' as Rilke advised his young poet.) I cannot be content merely to celebrate the city's beauty, to describe my emotions, to use expressions like 'La Serenissima' or 'the Floating City'. Impossible to write about the stagnant water of the canals, the melancholy of the sinking palaces, the cheerful humour of the Teatro Goldoni, the beauty to be found on every street corner. I could quote Thomas Mann, Philippe Sollers, Ezra Pound, Jean-Paul Sartre. But that wouldn't get me far. I could write a diatribe against mass tourism, the cruise ships depositing hundreds of visitors into the lagoon. I could mock the tourists as ugly, vulgar sheep. The tourist who fails to disguise the fact that he's a tourist is always an easy target. Unlike other recognisable types who proudly display their difference, the aesthetics of their tribe, the tourist is inelegance personified. The tourist hates the image that he gives of himself; he does not want to be lumped in with all the other tourists. What he wants is to be seen as someone he is not, i.e. a local. He wants to dissimulate his surprise, to conceal the fact that he's lost, that he's easy prey for pickpockets and con artists. The tourist is a touching character, particularly when he tries not to be seen with the guide he's paying to show him the 'secret Venice', 'off the beaten path'. In *Le vain travail de voir divers pays** Valery Larbaud gently pokes fun at tourists, who are stuck on the surface of things, permanently alienated from the reality

* 'The Fruitless Work of Seeing Various Countries'.

of the countries through which they travel. 'Yesterday, two old English ladies who wanted ice creams were only able to ask for ice, and I tried to help them by saying: "They call it gelato." "Oh: jaylar-tow! Thank you very much." And they got their ice creams, the dear old things. With no knowledge of Italian, their voyage must for them take on a cinematographic quality: an unfolding film of landscapes, streets, crowds, an entire life in which they can play no part.'

I land in Venice early in the afternoon. The water taxi drops me outside the Hotel Londra Palace, close to the Bridge of Sighs. It is seven in the evening, and in less than two hours I will be locked away. I walk through the city's most touristy quarters. I push my way through the crowds in St Mark's Square. Venice looks like a two-dimensional film set, and I can't help noticing how ugly the shopfronts are, how sad those expensive restaurants. In one square, I watch a man waving his arms around as he talks to a Dutch couple and their children. The tourists are wheeling heavy suitcases around, and the man is trying to explain, in pidgin English, that the noise of the suitcases disturbs the people who live there. When the Dutch woman finally understands, she puts her hand to her mouth and gestures at her husband to pick up the suitcases. The husband rolls his eyes as he obeys. He looks as though he thinks these Venetians are a bit oversensitive.

I find myself agreeing with the Hungarian novelist Sándor Márai, who wrote in his journal: 'It is not cities or landscapes that really interest me. In reality, my attention is always taken by human beings. For me, the spirit of Florence is not to be found in the Uffizi Gallery or the Boboli Gardens, but in a vision of an Englishwoman or a Tuscan cobbler in a narrow alley near Via Tornabuoni.'

I think about a trip I took to Kyoto a few years ago. In the Gion district, the tourists would rush after the geishas like paparazzi, trying to snap a photograph of them. Since then, I've heard that the city authorities have banned photography in that area. In Barcelona, anti-tourism protests recently turned violent. In tourist hotspots world-wide, groups of locals are rising up against the commodification of their home cities, arguing that their peace of mind is being sacrificed for dollars and euros. In Venice, more than any other place on earth, you are struck by what Patrick Deville calls 'the derealisation of the world, the rejection of history and geography'. The tourist is merely one consumer among many others who wants to 'do' Venice and bring back from his trip a series of selfies in which the city is nothing more than a picturesque backdrop. We are doomed to live in the empire of sameness, to eat in identical restaurants, to shop in the same boutiques on every continent. In the last thirty years, the population of Venice has declined by fifty per cent. Apartments here are rented out to visitors: twenty-eight million of them every year. The Venetians have become like Native Americans on a reservation, the last witnesses of a world dying before their eyes.

I walk amid the crowds. I understand that it is enough for me to be here, to let myself be caught up in the present. I feel happy, surprisingly serene.

In the midst of this multinational multitude, I no longer exist. I have the impression that I am disappearing, dissolving in the mass of humanity, and it is a delicious sensation. In *The Painter of Modern Life*, Baudelaire describes this feeling through the figure of Constantin Guys, 'a well-travelled, highly cosmopolitan artist':

> The crowd is his domain, as the air is to birds, as water is to fish. His passion and his profession is to marry the crowd. For the perfect *flâneur*, for the impassioned observer, there is an enormous pleasure to be found in the sheer numbers, in the undulating movements, in the ephemerality and infinity of crowds. Being outside oneself, and yet feeling at home everywhere; seeing the world, being at the centre of the world, and remaining hidden from the world.

I once experienced this sharpened attention to the present, this sense of *being there*, during a trip to India. I remember that the people I was with kept asking me about my impressions. They wanted to know how I was feeling, what I was gleaning from the landscape around me. What I thought of the people, whether I was shocked or enchanted by those sights so different from my usual daily surroundings. But I didn't say anything. I couldn't provide them with the remarks they were expecting on the poverty or the filth. Perhaps they took my silence for stupidity or indifference. In certain places – places overloaded with words and meanings, places where you feel obliged to experience this or that emotion – silence is the best reply. With this in mind, I walk through Venice. Palaces gleam in the slanting, orange sunlight. I explore the city in silence: a purely inner adventure. To appreciate the splendour, I seek neither to express it in words nor to capture it with my camera.

I sit down at a restaurant terrace. I order sardines, pasta with squash, veal Milanese, and some little clams cooked in parsley and garlic. I drink a glass of red wine. I would like to begin a conversation with the woman who serves me, who has purple bags under her big sad eyes. I would like to tell her that I'm ready to be locked away, and that, for once, I am not afraid. It's the outside world that frightens me: other people, their violence, their unrest. I have never been afraid of solitude. Besides, what is there to be scared of in an empty museum? Some psychopathic caretaker? Ghosts? I would love it if a ghost consented to appear before me. It's a novelist's dream: the chance to talk with spirits. How lucky I would feel if revenants came to whisper things in my ear. On this terrace, where I am starting to feel cold, I imagine seeing my dead loved ones again.

I walk through narrow, picturesque alleys. Above me, a sky teeming with stars. In Venice, the night is impenetrable: an anomaly in this age when everything is illuminated, transparent, when the concern for safety wins out over the charm of shadowy places. These days, in big cities, the sky never turns black. On a restaurant terrace, some couples are hugging, talking in low voices. The Dogana is not far away now. The only sounds I can hear are the click of my heels on the cobbles and the lapping of water against the hulls of moored boats. I am a young woman about to enter a convent.

I ring the doorbell of the museum. I wait for a long time, thinking that perhaps they have forgotten me, or that I'm late. I am about to walk away when a man opens the door.

'I'm Leïla – the writer who's supposed to sleep here tonight.'

He laughs. He seems to find the situation slightly absurd. He invites me inside, and I hear the door close heavily behind me.

The caretaker gives me a quick tour of the museum. He doesn't speak French and I don't speak Italian, but we can understand each other. To the right, he points to the toilets; to the left, the cafeteria and the small gift shop with its shelves of books on Venice and contemporary art. He hands me a catalogue, which includes a map of the museum.

From above, the Punta della Dogana resembles an icebreaker ship, with its pointed bow and its imposing warehouses, designed in the seventeenth century by Giuseppe Benoni. The building looks as though it's ready to slide into the water, to begin a voyage as a caravel crewed by sailors in search of adventure. Inside, the old and the new are intertwined. Tadao Andō, the Japanese architect who oversaw the renovation, decided to retain the building's original materials. The high ochre walls are made of trachyte – a stone typical of the streets of Venice – and covered in saltpetre. The building work was carried out using the '*scuci-cuci*' (stitch/unstitch) technique, which involves seeking out and replacing a damaged brick with a salvaged brick. So the past and the present, the ancient and the modern, old scars and young flesh, are mingled seamlessly upon the walls. The original roof has also been restored, with skylights added to let some natural light into the museum. Above me, I can see the building's immense wooden skeleton.

The museum as a whole, with a surface area of 5,000 square metres, gives an impression of austerity, emptiness. Inside this isosceles triangle, with its two equal sides both 105 metres long, the space is divided into nine naves, each ten metres wide. The most imposing space is in the centre: a large, square room with walls made from the Japanese architect's beloved concrete. I can easily imagine the age when this building was used as a customs house for merchandise arriving by sea. I can hear the noise of the cargo being unloaded, the voices of men at work, weighing, examining, packaging it all. I can see the ships – enormous caravels – mooring here, their holds full of spices, precious fabrics, exotic foodstuffs. The building is alive, eroded by nature. In places, on the walls, white flowers have grown. I feel as if I'm in the heart of a living organism. As if I've been swallowed by a whale.

The caretaker yanks me from my daydream. He seems in a rush to return to the comfort of his office. He gestures for me to follow him up the impressive concrete staircase. The glass banister continues along a sort of passageway and we reach the first floor. It is divided into smaller rooms, most of which have a window overlooking the stagnant waters of the canal. They have put my bed in a room displaying photographs by the American artist Berenice Abbott. It's a little camp bed whose orange covers match the orange walls.

The caretaker gives me an amused look. 'Okay?'

I nod and say: 'Yes, *grazie*, *grazie*, thank you very much.'

'*Buona notte*,' he says, before leaving me alone.

I have eaten too much and drunk too much.
What was I thinking? I've stuffed myself as if
afraid I might starve. As if I were setting off on a
long voyage. Now I feel like I'm going to throw
up. The wine has made me sleepy. That veal
Milanese was a really bad idea. I lie down on the
narrow, uncomfortable bed. So, am I just going
to spend the whole night here? I had been afraid
that I wouldn't sleep a wink, but already I feel
numb and drowsy. I would really like to smoke a
cigarette. I take one from the pack, grab a lighter
from my pocket, and for a few minutes, that is all
I can think about. In hotel rooms all over the
world, it has become impossible to smoke. The
windows don't open. In Asia, in the United
States, I have slept in rooms on the thirtieth floor
where the windows have thin horizontal stripes

to prevent you getting vertigo from looking down at the endless jungle of highways and skyscrapers. There are breathtaking views of soot-black horizons, but it's impossible to breathe the air outside. Sometimes, when I'm travelling, I will try little acts of subterfuge. I will turn on a fanlight in a bathroom, then stand on top of the toilet bowl or kneel on the window ledge. I will hold my arm outside and reach up with my lips, and what should be a pleasure – a guilty pleasure, obviously, but a pleasure all the same – turns into an acrobatic feat that leaves me feeling ridiculous. Once, in Zagreb, a woman watched me while I smoked a cigarette at the window. She was in a ground-floor apartment, and she called her husband over, then pointed up at me. Their children came to watch too, the whole family staring at me. I had no idea why. During the three days I spent in that room, each time I went to smoke a cigarette, the strange family would gather at their window and observe me suspiciously. I thought of writing a short story about it. I must have noted down the idea somewhere. One day, looking through a notebook, I will probably wonder what these words mean: 'Cigarette at the window, strange family, short story in a fantastical vein.'

In a museum, of course, it is not even worth thinking about. Here, the windows don't open, there are smoke detectors everywhere, and worst of all, there are cameras. Maybe the caretaker is observing me now from the control room? He must think me laughable, sitting here on my camp bed, still wearing my jacket. I would like to go and see him, ask him about his life as a museum caretaker, about his life full stop. In fact, I would be far more interested in finding out what he thinks of all these works he is paid to guard than I would in expressing my own opinion of them.

What kind of trap have I got myself into this time? Why did I agree to take part in this project when I am firmly convinced that writing must respond to a necessity, a private obsession, an inner urge? When journalists ask me why I chose this or that subject for a novel, I always struggle to come up with an answer. In the end, I make something up

– a plausible lie. If I told them it's the subjects that choose us, not the other way round, they would probably mark me down as pretentious or insane. But the truth is that my novels seek me out; they devour me. They're like a tumour growing inside me, taking control of my entire being, a cancer that can only be cured by abandoning myself to it. Can beauty flow from a text that isn't yours in the first place?

'Sleeping in a museum?' One of my friends made fun of the whole premise of this exercise. I tell myself I'm thick-skinned, but in fact I am very sensitive to criticisms of my work, the way I think, the projects I accept and the way I carry them out. My friend knew all that. He asked me what the point of it all was, what I could possibly write about, and he looked pleased with himself when I started stammering a few lame justifications.

'It's a sort of performance. An existential experience.' I invented all sorts of rubbish, trying to give some meaning to a choice that I was already regretting.

'Surely there's something more interesting a writer could be doing than going to sleep in a museum!' my friend said. 'Writers should be outside, talking about the world, giving a voice to people who never get heard. I'm going to be honest with you: this whole night-at-the-museum thing seems pretty pointless and pretentious to me.'

I wonder what I'm supposed to do. Walk around? Look at each artwork and hope something inspires me? I am chilled, petrified by this obligation, and I now feel so exhausted that I just want to go to bed and dream. *But this is not a hotel room*, I tell myself. I sit up, open my eyes wide. *Come on, be reasonable – you can't go to bed yet. You just got here! You really think you're here just to sleep? You have something to do: a book to write.*

I admire people who say they are not afraid of anything. I am fascinated by people who demonstrate physical and moral courage, who do not fear conflict, who don't suddenly start running down the street, spooked by some irrational panic. I am not like that – I'm a fearful person – yet I feel protected in this place, this sanctuary. I like being locked up in the darkness of a cinema. I am not afraid in libraries, in bookshops, in small local museums that you visit less for the quality of the exhibits than because they are somewhere you can warm up on a cold day. The rest of the time, I'm afraid. Perhaps it's because I was raised by a permanently worried mother whose catchphrase was: 'Be careful!'. A mother who saw risk everywhere: injuring yourself, catching your death of cold, falling into the hands of a predator. Back then, I was annoyed with her for being so anxious. I felt as if she were trying to stop me living my life. When I had children, I realised I was being unfair. I understood the terror that gripped her, that paralysed her, because I felt the same thing myself. Sometimes I dream that I have trapped my children inside a glass jar that will protect them from everything, that will make them invincible, keep them out of harm's way forever.

In Paris, the room I use as an office is small and gloomy, like a nest. I like writing with the door shut, the curtains drawn. Many of my writer friends – mostly men – tell me that, for them, writing is inseparable from motion. They go jogging in the forest or on city boulevards; they go for long, late-afternoon walks. It's a classic theme in literature, from Montaigne to Murakami, via Jean-Jacques Rousseau. I'm not sure I know how to walk like that. I do not have the soul of a *flâneuse*, strolling aimlessly, cheerfully, with no destination in mind. I am afraid of men who might follow me. Joggers who might jump on me. I often turn around when I hear footsteps behind me. I never walk down streets I don't know. The first time I took the RER suburban train in Paris, the man sitting opposite me unzipped his trousers and stared at me while he masturbated. Another man, late one night, stuck his foot in the door of my apartment building, and I was only saved because a male neighbour arrived there at the same time as I did. For a long time, I wished I could be invisible. I dreamed up ploys and envied boys, who did not suffer from such fears. If I tend to remain cloistered, avoiding the outside world, it is perhaps less so I can write than because I am terrified. Often, I wonder what my life would have been like without this fear. If I'd been a brave, intrepid adventurer capable of facing terrible dangers. 'We belong to the gender of fear,' writes Virginie Despentes in *King Kong Theory*.

In this museum, I have no fear, but I do feel ill at ease, clumsy. It's obvious to me that I am out of place here, that I am a problem the museum could do without, that I am disturbing the sleep of someone or something. Perhaps, as in a fairy tale, the objects here come to life when night falls and there is no one left to observe them. Perhaps the paintings stretch out and move along the walls;

perhaps ghosts emerge from the sculptures that they inspired and fictional characters come to life. But I am there, an irritating witness, a cumbersome somebody in the way of all the magic, preventing the nocturnal parade from taking place. I take off my shoes because the sound of my heels on the floor is bothering me. I would like to make myself as small as possible.

I decide to walk barefoot around the museum, to follow the itinerary that any ordinary visitor might follow: someone who goes to the counter, buys a ticket, and conscientiously moves from artwork to artwork, observing them carefully, reading the explanatory labels, trying to grasp what the artist was trying to say. I don't know much about contemporary art. Unlike books, art was a late arrival in my life. In my grandmother's house, the walls were covered with dubious daubings: desperately sad still lifes, bouquets of flowers in faded colours, and – most imposing of all – a bombastic portrait of my grandfather in his Spahi uniform, which hung above the fireplace. My parents were interested in contemporary Moroccan artists. I remember the naive characters painted by Chaïbia and the works of Abbès Saladi, whose monstrous creatures with the heads of birds or horses haunted my childhood nightmares. My father painted too, and at the end of his life, when he was no longer working and was prey to melancholy, he produced some very beautiful pictures. Black skies, ripped apart by storms. Stony deserts, heavy with sorrow. After his time in prison, he painted characters with diving helmets for heads. I have a photograph of him, sitting on the floor in a friend's studio. His fingers are covered with red paint, his face is turned to the camera, and he looks happy. But I don't think we ever talked about art together.

In the 1980s, there was no museum in Rabat. As a child, I never went to see an exhibition, and the art world seemed to me something reserved for the elite, another world. At the time, art was still seen through a Western prism and those Moroccan artists that my parents liked did not have the visibility they have acquired, with the twenty-first century's vogue for African art. Of the great paintings and famous sculptures, I saw only reproductions in my history books or in exhibition catalogues that my parents brought home from abroad.

I knew the names of Picasso, Van Gogh and Botticelli, but I had no idea what I might feel if I stood in front of one of their paintings. While novels were intimate, accessible objects, which I bought at a bookshop near my school and devoured in my bedroom, art was a distant land, its works hidden behind the high walls of European museums. My culture revolved around literature and cinema, and that perhaps explains why I became obsessed with fiction at such a young age.

The first few times I visited a museum after moving to Paris, I was impressed but ill at ease, just as I was at the theatre – another rare experience in Morocco, and one which requires some getting used to, I think, in order to be truly appreciated. In museums, I would observe other people. When they stood for a long time in front of a painting, I would do the same, assuming this one must be more important than the others. Ever the diligent student, I would read the plaques and try to memorise the title of the painting, the school to which the artist belonged. I wondered if I too, one day, would be able to utter phrases like: 'What a colourist!' or 'What mastery of perspective!'

When I was twenty-five, I took a trip to Italy with a friend who'd been to art school. He accompanied me to the Uffizi, which I was visiting for the first time, and in front of each painting I would try to look thoughtful, as solemn as a child at her First Communion, reverential in the face of such beauty and genius. My friend made fun of me for my uniform deference, my total lack of discrimination and critical faculty. 'Don't look so in awe of everything,' he said. 'Just enjoy the stuff that you really like, the stuff that moves you.'

Since then, I've been lucky enough to visit many galleries and I've always tried to follow my friend's advice. I would like to be a pleasure-seeker, guided only by my personal taste and my emotions. But the truth is that feeling of unease has not completely dissipated. To me, museums continue to seem like towering, impressive places, fortresses of beauty and genius that make me feel small in comparison. I feel alienated when I am inside a museum, distanced from the art in a way I try to conceal by feigning nonchalance. For me, museums remain a bastion of Western elitism, speaking a language I don't fully understand.

I begin walking around the Punta della Dogana, catalogue in hand. The featured exhibition is entitled *Luogo e Segni*, 'Place and signs'. It brings together thirty-six artists whose works question man's relationship with nature, and the artist's ability to capture the poetry of the world, to reveal the memory of objects and the presence among us of ghosts and the dead. The two curators of the exhibition have also tried to emphasise the connections between the artists themselves: their personal friendships, their mutual inspirations. One artist in particular is pre-eminent: the Lebanese painter and poet Etel Adnan, whose works are shown in several rooms and whose poems we can hear being read out by the American theatre director Robert Wilson. Born in Beirut in 1925, Etel Adnan studied at Harvard, then moved to California. Her first books, *Arab Apocalypse* and *Sitt Marie Rose*, made her a major figure in the pacifism movement and the protests against the wars in Lebanon, then Vietnam. I discovered her almost ten years ago, when I read an interview with her in a French newspaper. At the time, I was blown away by the wisdom of her words, by the power of her descriptions of her work as an artist and a writer. The heir to a great Arab tradition, she saw writing and painting as twin disciplines, each feeding off the other. Her paintings – abstract landscapes in bright colours, as pure as childhood visions – enchanted me with their intense beauty. She painted them while looking out at hills from her window in California. Or she summoned a buried memory from her childhood in Greece, in Lebanon, and tried to bring back to life her dead mother and other lost loved ones. What also struck me was what she said about identity. Like me, she grew up in an Arab country, as part of a French-speaking family. Afterwards, she emigrated to the United States; all her life, she lived in the country of others. About the Arabic language, at once so familiar and so strange to her, she said: 'I found myself at the door of that language. Even though I could speak it in the street, I would be incapable of using it to write a poem. So I built a myth around it as a sort of paradise lost.'

On the wall facing me, I notice a line of dark-coloured panels. I read that these 'photograms' were created by exposing photosensitive paper to moonlight. I move closer and stare at them for a long time, but all I see are some large, dark panels. Further on, a block of marble also contains a frag-ment of moon, because it was exposed to the light of that heavenly body one night in August 2019. On the floor, there's a white balloon. Just an ordi-nary balloon, like the ones I blow up for my chil-dren's birthday parties, and which I like to burst with a pin after the guests have departed. This balloon contains the breath of two artists, and is no doubt intended as a metaphor for love and the passing of time. But all I see is a block of stone and a rubber balloon. Unable to perceive anything beyond the banality of the object itself, I feel a little guilty. I must be stupid. Either that or the heaviness of the veal Milanese in my stomach is preventing me from mustering the necessary mental effort. In one of the rooms, the floor is covered in a sort of glittery powder. If I lean down and blow on it, will anyone notice? I imagine visiting this room with my son, who would undoubtedly want to leave a footprint in the iridescent sand.

I am not about to start accusing these artists of being cons. I can't claim to have anything interesting to say about what they are doing. Besides, I would hardly be the first to denigrate modern art on that basis. What could be more banal than attacking supposedly conceptual works of art? Perhaps this is a sign of my own lack of imagination, or perhaps it is connected to the fact that I am a writer, and that every book, for me, is synonymous with a long, drawn-out struggle with myself, but the simplicity of certain artworks leaves me disconcerted.

Marcel Duchamp said that it was the viewer who made the artwork. Following that logic, it is not the artwork that lacks quality or interest; it is the viewer who doesn't know how to see it properly. Yves Michaud quotes Duchamp in 'L'art à l'état gazeux'*: 'When I say the viewer, I do not mean only the contemporary viewer, but all of posterity and all viewers of works of art who, with their opinions, decide if something will remain or survive because it has a depth that the artist produced, without knowing it. The artist likes to believe that he is completely aware of what he is doing, why he is doing it, how he is doing it, and the intrinsic value of his work. But I don't believe any of that. I sincerely believe that the painting is made as much by the viewer as by the artist.' So it isn't the object that matters, but the resultant experience. It is through the magic of looking, through interactivity, that an object becomes a work of art. Agreed. But it is precisely because art can be anywhere, in a urinal or a slice of cake, that contemporary artists and the people around them are so defensive about their work. This insularity protects them from the obvious risk of dilution, or even ridicule. The less the work itself is the product of a complex technique

* 'Art in a Gaseous State'.

or long period of work, the greater the need to create this circle of 'connoisseurs' to validate it: *Yes, this really is art.* And if, one day, I am admitted into that inner circle, if I in turn become an initiate, perhaps I too will end up saying: 'No, you idiot, it's not just a balloon. It's art!'

I sit on a stone bench, close to the entrance of the museum. I observe these vast, cold rooms and am filled with sadness. I feel like I'm at a party where I don't belong, where nobody knows me. For a moment, I am so downcast that I think about running upstairs and lying down on my camp bed. If I hid inside my sleeping bag, I wouldn't have to watch the hours of the night tick by; all my anxieties would be dissolved in sleep.

Instead, I stand up and walk through a room, across the centre of which is a long red plastic bead curtain. Like blood pouring from the ceiling on to the floor. A rain of tears, a haemorrhage, a sunset. I walk through it again and again. The beads, when you move them, make a sound like little bells. There was a curtain like this at the grocer's where my younger sister and I used to buy chocolate caramels. All I'd have to do, I think, is tug lightly on one of those threads and it would snap. Then I'd hear the beads rolling around on the floor, just like when you break a necklace and the pearls spill everywhere. How long would it take before the caretaker came running? He would probably be bewildered, having to deal with a writer turned vandal in the middle of the night.

The curtain is a work by Felix González-Torres, who died of AIDS in 1996. I stand back a little and observe the big room through this red shimmer. I see the hot liquid spreading, and disease coming into my life while I can do nothing to stop it. I have always been obsessed by my body, which I carry around like a burden. This body that hinders me, makes me vulnerable; this body that seems to be secretly conspiring against me. Perhaps my blood is contaminated too. Inside me, unknown to me, some unstoppable disaster might even now be brooding. I think: *My body will kill me*, and I laugh all alone in this room, so empty that my laughter echoes from its walls. It's strange, but the face of

Adèle, the heroine of my first novel, comes to my mind. Adèle, who likes to be mistreated, who wants her body to be punished, beaten, just so that she can feel something. She perceives the world through a curtain of blood, but nobody else sees it the way she does. As a young girl, I became aware of what Kundera calls 'the monotony of corporeal life'. The sadness of our organic functions, the ugliness of naked flesh, the helplessness to which we are reduced by disease . . . all of this continues to obsess me and to be a central theme in my work.

I am not afraid of death. Death is nothing more than final, complete, absolute solitude. It is the end of conflicts and misunderstandings. It is also a return to the truth of things, a stripping away. What I fear is the body's resistance. Degradation. Physical pain. When Tolstoy was an old, sick man, his mind tormented by endless rows with his wife, he fled the famous house at Yasnaya Polyana, with which all his books are associated. He left for an unknown destination and he died in the apartment of the stationmaster at Astapovo train station. His body was sent back to his family in a wooden crate bearing these simple words: 'Contents: corpse.'

On the wall of this room is a work by Roni Horn: some metal bars, with Emily Dickinson poems printed on them. A famous recluse, Dickinson lived for years in complete isolation, refusing to be part of the world or to publish her writing.

And I dreamed of being locked up. Of living only there, in those few square metres, in books, in words, in the smell of my dreams. Of setting my own pace. Of being totally free.

> *They shut me up in Prose*
> *As when a little Girl*
> *They put me in the Closet*
> *Because they liked me still*

Roni Horn was a friend of Felix González, and one of the aims of the exhibition is to highlight these artistic friendships. The two of them would visit museums and spend whole afternoons walk-ing together. Inside the 'cube' – a monumental concrete room designed by Tadao Andō – there are some big glass blocks, a work by Roni Horn entitled *Well and Truly*. These blocks look like enormous mint sweets, or like hand-carved icebergs. Like running water petrified by magic. It is night now, and the blocks are lit only by artificial light, giving them an unreal atmosphere. Depending on whether you lean forward or stand up straight, the gleam of the polished surface takes on pinkish or bluish shades. It seems possible that, were I to touch them, they would turn liquid again; my hand would sink inside, a puddle would form on the ground and I could swim in it. In a troubling, melancholic way, they realise the fantasy of grasping the ungraspable. Of becoming a magician. Water, snow, wind, cannot be held in your hand. No matter how hard you try to capture them, they always slip through your fingers. This is quite similar to what every writer feels when beginning a novel. As you advance, a world is created, but the essential vision remains inaccessible, as if in writing you are at the same time giving up on what you really wanted to write. Writing is an experience of continual failure, unsurpassable frustration, absolute impossibility. And yet we do it anyway. We write. 'To keep your courage while knowing in advance that you will be defeated, and to go into battle: that is literature,' said the Chilean novelist Roberto Bolaño. I am often asked what literature can do. It's like asking a doctor what medicine can do. The more I go on, the more powerless I feel. That powerlessness obsesses me, devours me. I write blindly, uncomprehendingly, inexplicably.

In the middle of the museum stand some massive black monoliths, lit from within. Through the smoked windows of these giant terrariums, I can glimpse the branches and leaves of night-blooming jasmine, also known as *mesk el arabi*. I walk between these terrariums as in a forest of glass where nature is held prisoner. I know that tree well. In Morocco, its flower is familiar, sung of by poets and lovers. It has the strongest scent in the plant kingdom and – like the datura, another tree that fascinated me as a child – its flowers open only at night. Nature plays some strange tricks. The flowers appear only after dark, as if the tree wished to preserve its beauty, keep it secret, shelter it from prying eyes, just as I dream of remaining detached from the world. Its scent can be smelled only at night. Is this a way of communicating with nocturnal insects? Is it because perfumes reveal their truest power, their greatest depth, in darkness? Hicham Berrada, who created this installation, decided to invert the plant's natural cycle. During the day, the terrarium remains opaque and the jasmine is plunged into darkness, but its scent fills the museum. At night, on the other hand, the sodium lighting reproduces the conditions of a sunny summer day. Everything is reversed, turned upside down; the artist becomes demiurge, sorcerer's apprentice, illusionist. I think of what Chekhov said about great writers: they are those who make it snow in the middle of summer and who describe the snowflakes so vividly that you shiver with cold.

In Rabat, there was a night-blooming jasmine near the front door of our house. In summer, at nightfall, we would leave the window open to create draughts, and my father would say: 'Can you smell it? That's the night-blooming jasmine!' Year after year, it never ceased to amaze him. All I have to do is close my eyes, and I can remember that sweet, heady scent. Tears well in my eyes. So here they are at last, the ghosts. And there it is, the smell of the country of my childhood, vanished, swallowed up by time.

My name is Night. That's what Leïla means, in Arabic. But I doubt that is enough to explain the attraction I felt, from a very early age, for nocturnal life. In the daytime, everyone behaves in expected ways. People want to keep up appearances, make themselves look virtuous, polite, obedient. As a child, it seemed to me that the daytime hours were devoted to trivial, repetitive activities. It was the realm of boredom and obligations. Then the night arrived. We went to bed, and I suspected that, while we slept, other actors entered the stage. People expressed themselves in a different way. Women were beautiful; they pulled back their hair and exposed their gleaming, perfumed skin. There was something fragile about them when they drank too much and laughed, but at the same time an invincible power seemed to emanate from them. These metamorphoses enthralled me. And when I was old enough to go out, or even just before then, a sort of rage took hold of me. An urgency, a hunger that drove me to explore the night myself. I didn't want to be a good little girl.

The night-blooming jasmine is the smell of my lies, my adolescent loves, cigarettes smoked in secret, forbidden parties. It is the scent of freedom. The tree was there, just outside the iron door that I opened, as quietly as I could, to sneak out and meet my friends. Powerful in the darkness, evanescent at dawn. As a teenager, I discovered bars, cabarets, nightclubs, parties at a beach hut, the dark and empty streets of my torpid capital. At a certain hour of the night, the good girls would go home and the others would appear. Back then, prostitutes fascinated me, aroused me, moved me. In a cabaret near Mohammedia, fat, lecherous men would sit watching flabby-thighed women dance on stage. The men would beckon the women over to sit on their knees, pour them a glass of cheap whisky, kiss them on the neck. I remember a woman who undressed in front of me in the toilets of a bar in Tangier, laughing at how nasty and stupid her clients were.

I was intoxicated by my freedom and, at the same time, I was afraid. I told myself I would be punished for not knowing my place. That if anything happened to me, I would have asked for it. At night, when the boys had fun driving cars the wrong way along the motorway between Rabat and Casablanca, I used to think: *You mustn't die, because it would kill Maman*. But, like Blanche in *A Streetcar Named Desire*, I could often count on the generosity of strangers. One night, at a bar in Casablanca, I was waiting for some friends and I was the only girl there. The barman told me I should always sit at the counter, as close as possible to whoever was serving drinks. 'The secret,' he told me, 'is to have your own lighter. If you ask a man for a light, he'll think you want to talk to him, and that'll make him believe he has a chance with you. Then you won't be able to get rid of him. So, if you smoke, always carry a lighter.'

That world has disappeared. And I don't want to defile it. Perhaps it will become a novel one day, because only literature can bring those vanished lives back into the light. It's been twenty years since I left my native country, and I feel a sort of melancholy; I have the impression that I have forever distanced myself from the sensations of my childhood.

'I'm not ashamed of the way I am. I can't be any different from how I've always been. Until eighteen, all I'd known was a tidy apartment in a tidy bourgeois provincial town, and school, school, school . . . Real life was happening beyond seven walls,' says Helena, the heroine of Milan Kundera's *The Joke*.

I was raised like an indoor cat. I never played any sport. I can't ride a bicycle, and I do not have a driving licence. As a child, I spent most of my time at home. I studied. Nothing much happened in Rabat, and my sisters and I would entertain ourselves by reading books and watching films. It wasn't only the night that was a forbidden land, it was outside. Girls did not belong in the streets, in city squares, on café terraces – where, I remember, all the customers were men. A girl who was travelling had to go straight from point A to point B. Any deviation from that line, and she was a slut, a bad influence, a lost soul. There were so many dangers: getting pregnant, falling in love, failing in school because she was too busy mooning over some boy. These possibilities were described to me as a series of falls, each one more devastating than the last. Girls were Eve for all eternity.

With adolescence came dreams of escape, desires for freedom, for nights without a chaperone, for streets where I could look at others and they could look at me. Since it was forbidden to me, movement became, in my mind, synonymous with liberty. Freeing myself meant fleeing, getting out of the prison that was my home. I didn't want to become a 'housewife'. In my final year of school, our philosophy teacher, who liked to smoke in class and give lessons in the garden, explained to us that existing consisted simultaneously of escaping the self and leaving home. There could be no individuality, no freedom, without a wrench. You had to flee every compartment that closed you in while giving the illusion of comfort. You had to

beware the 'gentrification of the heart'; better to
be a nomad, a wanderer, a compulsive traveller.
And I – who, at eighteen, had until then been
content to go from school to home, from home to
my grandparents' farm – I dreamed, with a mixture
of fear and excitement, of a place where I might
truly belong. I wanted to conquer the outside
world.

Now, alone and barefoot in this museum, I
wonder why I was so desperate to be locked up
in here. How could the feminist, the activist, the
writer I aspire to be, how could she fantasise
about four walls and a firmly shut door? I should
want to break all the cages, blow on the castle
walls until they shake and crumble. Writing
cannot consist solely of withdrawing, taking
pleasure in the warmth of an apartment, building
brick walls to protect yourself from the outside,
and never looking anyone in the eye. It must also
involve nurturing dreams of expansion, conquest,
getting to know the world, the Other, the
unknown. What can you cultivate inside a fortress,

other than indifference? Peace and quiet is a self-ish fantasy.

'When Allah created the earth, my father told me, he had good reasons to separate men and women [. . .] Order and harmony exist only when each group respects the *hudud*. Any transgression inevitably brings anarchy and misfortune. But women would think constantly of breaking the rules. They were obsessed by the world that existed beyond the front gate. All day long, they would fantasise about prancing through imaginary streets.' This is from the opening paragraph of *Dreams of Trespass*, a novel by Moroccan sociologist Fatema Mernissi about her childhood in a harem in the medina of Fez. In this book, she describes how women were kept in confinement, guarded by a man with a bunch of keys hanging from his belt. The man would lock the heavy wooden door every night. Girls in that era were told that the world was divided by invisible boundaries, the *hudud*, and that anyone who crossed those boundaries would be guilty of bringing dishonour on their clan.

I did not grow up in a harem, and no one ever stopped me living my life. But I am the product of that world, and my great-grandmothers were women who believed in the necessity of those boundaries. No doubt they dreamed, in their small, confined spaces, of a greater, more abundant life. My Alsatian grandmother, who was something of an anomaly within Moroccan society, made a strong impression, with her desire for adventure, with her courage and tenacity. I never suffered what my ancestors went through, but all the same, the idea persisted, even in my childhood, that women were immobile, sedentary beings, that it was safer to keep them inside than to let them out. They had less value than men. They inherited less. A woman was always somebody's wife or daughter. My father was often pitied for having only daughters. Even in her sixties, my aunt didn't dare smoke in front of her brother, because it is well-known that women who smoke have no virtue. My parents wanted us to be free, independent women, capable of expressing our own opinions, making our own choices. But neither they nor we could be indifferent to the context in which we grew up, or to those 'invisible laws' that governed public spaces. So they always warned us to be cautious and discreet when we left the welcoming walls of our home.

In Paul Morand's novel *The Man in a Hurry*, the narrator talks to himself: 'Pierre, think carefully before you fall asleep and before you wake up a homeowner. Pierre, you'll put on weight. You're taking root. You're becoming immobile. Remember, some snails are crushed to death by the weight of their own shells.' Because I was a woman, I was always afraid of the shell that would crush me. Afraid of taking root. I didn't want to be Penelope, left behind, waiting for her adventurous lover to return. It seems to me that existence is nothing other than an attempt to destroy the wildness within us, to rein us in, to control our instincts. This perhaps explains my literary obsession with the torments of domestic life. At some point in all my novels, the mothers feel – however fleetingly and shamefully – the desire to abandon their children. Each of them is nostalgic for the woman she used to be before becoming someone's mother. They suffer from that compulsion to build a nest, a safe and comfortable home for their children, a doll's house in which they will be the smiling prisoners. You must be 'there' for them, we are told. You must 'know your place'.

Virginia Woolf, more than anyone, truly understood the degree to which the condition of women forced them to live in a constant tension between the inside and the outside. They were refused not only the comfort and privacy of a room of their own, but also the vastness of the outside world where they might have mixed with others and had adventures. The question of women is a question of space. It is impossible to understand the domination women are subjected to without studying its geography, without evaluating the constraints imposed upon their bodies by clothing, by places, by other eyes. Rereading Virginia Woolf's diary, I remembered that she had once imagined a sequel to *A Room of One's Own*. The provisional title was . . . *The Open Door*.

I sit on my orange camp bed and examine the photographs on the walls: a series entitled *Changing New York*. They are the work of Berenice Abbott, an American photographer born in 1898 in Ohio, who later became Man Ray's assistant. In the 1920s, she lived in Paris, where she discovered the work of Eugène Atget. When he died, she bought his archives. Atget had spent years photographing different parts of Paris with the impossible ambition of creating an exhaustive document of the capital in the throes of transformation. In 1929, Abbott returned to New York. The city she found was barely recognisable as the one she had left behind. In the space of a few years, the nineteenth-century buildings had been demolished to make way for a new age of glass and steel. Perhaps she felt then what I feel whenever I go back to

Morocco: the strange impression that the most intimate, most familiar world has been evolving in my absence, that it has been transformed. It feels simultaneously like a dazzling magic trick and a betrayal.

Abbott adopted a deeply paradoxical approach: to photograph change, to immobilise transformation, to immortalise all those places as they were swallowed up by time. Like Atget, she wanted to capture metamorphosis in an image. What she photographed was a dying world, and another one that was being born in its place. In the pictures on my wall, the pale grey buildings are like palimpsests. In their concrete flesh, they bear witness to the past. I move closer. All the artists in this exhibition seem obsessed by this same quest: to bring to light the memory contained in each object, even the most banal and insignificant. To find some trace of ghosts in the world around them, and in that way to prove that nothing ever completely dies. That the whole world is covered with scars. All these artists shared the impossible ambition of grasping the ungraspable.

I always try to look behind the banality of objects to find the prayers and memories they contain. I like mundane, kitsch objects, the ugly little things that we keep despite everything because they remind us of a memory. I like lucky charms, amulets. I love visiting the apartments of writers or people I admire. I cried when I saw Dostoyevsky's samovar, Pushkin's lock of hair, and Victor Hugo's writing desk. These silent, motionless witnesses move me; they make me sentimental.

It has been twenty years since I left my homeland. Sometimes, I am asked what I think of this exile, but I always reject the word. I am not in exile. I wasn't forced to leave or driven out by circumstances. In Paris, I found what I had gone there in search of: the freedom to live life the way I wanted, to sit for hours on a café terrace drinking wine, reading and smoking. I'm an immigrant, a metic, not in the usual derogatory French sense of the term *métèque*, but in the neutral etymological sense of someone who has left their own city to live in another. Each time I go back to Rabat, I cannot help but notice the changes to my city. Some of the places I used to go when I was young

have disappeared, while others have been transformed. Apartment blocks and bourgeois houses
have been built on what was once wasteland. By
the Bou Regreg river, the marshes that used to
attract mosquitoes and birds have been reclaimed,
and the ice-cream vendor has sold his shop to a
mobile phone company. The Italian restaurant
where I would sometimes eat dinner with my
parents is still there, in a dark city-centre street.
The menu hasn't changed, but the waiter, now
very elderly, has hearing problems.

I have not kept much from those days. The
bedroom where I spent my childhood was emptied
in my absence. I wasn't able to salvage anything:
no schoolbooks or toys, no photographs or clothes.
At the time, I felt as if my past had been profaned,
that I had been robbed. And then, with the passing
years, I began to feel an immense relief. A few
months ago, I realised that I had lost letters, an old
ring, a pen belonging to my father. I lost access to
the mailbox I'd been using on my computer, and
ten years of correspondence completely vanished.
I had kept copies of a few photographs from my
adolescence on a USB stick, but now that too is

lost. I went through all the drawers in my office; I flew into a rage; I even prayed, as my grandmother advised me, to St Anthony of Padua. But it made no difference. Once I had calmed down, I felt as if I had been relieved of a burden. As if God, in stealing these precious objects from me, had in fact been doing me a favour.

I go into the next room, where some large canvases are hung. *Api e petrolio fanno luce* ('Bees and Oil Make Light') was created using wax from candles burned by churchgoers in Rome. The artist, Alessandro Piangiamore, melted the wax before colouring and moulding it. The picture evokes a stormy summer sky, the restless parade of clouds, the thunder about to rumble. Whites and blues are intermingled, the heights dark, the hollows filled with light. From a distance, it looks like a painting, but as you approach, you begin to see the granular, supple material of the melted candles. If I listen closely, perhaps I will hear the murmured prayers? 'Make him well again', 'Make him love me again', 'Lord, protect my children'. How many secrets, how many memories, are trapped within this ex-voto artwork? Its beauty calms me. I would like to scratch my nails against the canvas, feel that contact with the wax the way I used to as a kid when I would dig my fingers into a lit candle to leave my fingerprints on it. I would like to believe; I would like to pray. But I don't know how to do that. I think of what Roland Barthes wrote in his *Mourning Diary*: 'I see swallows soar through the summer evening air. And I think [. . .] how barbarous not to believe in souls – in the immortality of souls! The idiotic truth of materialism!'

Inside a glass display case, the *leporello* designed by Etel Adnan is entitled *Dhikr*, which can be translated as 'incantation'. *Leporelli* were originally little books, folded accordion-style, in which Japanese artists would draw in ink. Here, Adnan has written, in various colours, the same word: 'Allah'. She wrote it again and again, each time a bomb exploded in Beirut. Like a child praying under the bombardments, like a believer clinging to her faith when meaning collapses, when violence destroys everything. Around the sacred word, she draws half-moons and stars, multicoloured constellations, opening up infinity to people crushed by war. Offering them breathing space.

I sit on the freezing floor and close my eyes. I remember the calls to prayer I used to hear, in the middle of the night, from my house in Rabat. The voice of the muezzin would half-wake me: it seemed so close, and I knew that in our house others were waking too. I imagined the believers leaving their homes, their faces thick with sleep, walking in the dark streets and entering the mosque, carrying their prayer mats.

I hear the distant, muffled notes of Tchaikovsky's *Pathétique Symphony*. Behind a forest of brick columns, there's a screen. A woman is walking through the streets of Sarajevo under siege; she is a musician on her way to join her fellow orchestra members. I hear the sound of her heels on the concrete, and her breath, heavy with anxiety and impatience. Her breathing is like a metronome in that war-torn city, that suffocating city with its terrified inhabitants. Her chest rises. She stops, frozen by the coming danger. Then she runs across empty crossroads bathed in sunlight. She passes other people, all looking vigilant, worried. They are dressed in black and grey. At the time, people were advised not to wear red or any other bright colour, because it made you an easier target for snipers. This was what the blockade meant to the artist Anri Sala: *1395 Days Without Red*. In this film, he reconstructs those anxious days and pays tribute to the Sarajevo Philharmonic Orchestra, who continued performing during the siege, transforming their art into a weapon of resistance, a cry for humanity. What traces remain in Sarajevo of those days of suffocation? Perhaps that is the artist's mission: to exhume the past, to save it from oblivion, to create this diabolical dialogue between past and present. To refuse burial.

In an interview with Hans Ulrich Obrist, Etel Adnan says:

It is very important to actively remember, even more than it was in the past when memory preserved itself. We live in a city where we used to have libraries, museums, friends. There was already a memory in its stones and in the people who knew them. Today, we are constantly faced with the void. Entire cities have been destroyed. Before the war, we didn't need to think about Beirut because Beirut was there. But the Beirut of the 1960s has disappeared. If memory does not preserve it, that city will be wiped off the map. This applies to other places too. Including France, where things have changed so much that we no longer even know how to read those that have survived. We no longer see cathedrals the way those who built them saw them. It requires a considerable cultural effort to see – it is not because a building stands before us that we are necessarily able to see it.

Notre-Dame went up in flames yesterday. When I landed in Venice today, the man who was driving my water taxi asked me how the cathedral was, the way someone might enquire after a beloved, ailing grandparent. What Etel Adnan tells us is that cities die, just as people, animals and plants die. Cities and buildings disappear, taking with them the emotions of those who loved, walked, knew them. In a letter to his lover Franco Farolfi in 1941, Pier Paolo Pasolini describes a night spent in Paderno with his friend Paria. A night of laughter surrounded by nature, 'amid orchards and cherry trees laden with fruit'. A night when 'an enormous number of fireflies formed groves of light'. Thirty years later, in another letter, he explains that pollution has killed off the fireflies: 'It was such a sudden, devastating phenomenon.' To Pasolini, the fireflies had been killed by consumer society, unfettered capitalism, the destruction of nature for profit; and along with those luminous insects had gone the memory of his nights spent at one with the natural world. Beauty is dead, he seems to say, sacrificed on the altar of money. Consumer society leads to the disappearance of popular cultures and the disintegration of the landscape. 'And so everything that, for centuries on end, seemed like it could last forever – that *could* have lasted forever – is now starting to fall apart. Venice is dying.' Moreover, he added: 'When a child does not feel loved, he decides unconsciously to die, and that is what happens. Stone, wood, colour: these are becoming things of the past.' I wonder if Notre-Dame took her own life. Exhausted by all those who wanted to consume her, perhaps the cathedral set fire to herself? Notre-Dame died of overexposure: seen by too many pairs of eyes, after becoming merely an object for tourist consumption.

Venice, too, is dying. To look upon it is to look upon the death throes of a city. Through the window, I see the waters that will soon swallow it up. I try to imagine the tottering stilts on which it stands. I picture its palaces buried in water and mud, its memories of glory forgotten by all, its cobbled squares reduced to nothingness. Venice carries within it the seeds of its own destruction, and it is perhaps this fragility that gives it its splendour.

On the television last night, someone was saying that the emotion stirred by the Notre-Dame fire was testimony to the return of religious feeling in France. But it seems to me that the exact opposite is true. If we weep, it's because we live in a society desperately lacking in transcendence, the desire to elevate itself; one lacking any kind of nobility whatsoever. We weep for God's deafening silence. I grew up in a country where religion occupied an important place in everyone's existence. A country where God was invited into all the spaces of everyday life, into every verbal expression. God sees all and chooses our fate. Back then, it bothered me a great deal that I had no faith. It was like a handicap that ostracised me, prevented me from being one with the people I loved. I wished I could feel something, could submit to something greater than myself. I dreamed of being granted a vision one night, like Blaise Pascal on his night of fire. God would appear to me and save me from fear. But my great night never came, and my desire for transcendence was only ever fulfilled by literature. Sometimes I think that, faced with the fading of religious faith, or its hijacking by obscurantist fanatics, literature might serve as the sacred word. It might elevate us. In Beirut, I spent a day with the Lebanese poet Salah Stétié. Rarely have I encountered anyone with such faith in the power of poetry and literature. For him, they represented transcendence in a world where religions had been corrupted and our gods betrayed. If we could no longer believe in anything, there was always poetry, which – according to Stétié – would never die.

Through a skylight, I catch a glimpse of the statue of Fortune atop the building. At the peak of the Customs House's corner tower, there are two giants carrying a golden globe, on which Fortune stands. She is wearing a veil, which moves in the wind, and playing the role of weather vane. 'Islam stems from this culture in which everyone is convinced that everything is doomed for destruction,' adds Etel Adnan. '[. . .] Arabs live ephemeral lives; it is perhaps this that makes them more modern than they themselves realise.' Arab culture, and particularly Arab poetry, are steeped in nomadism, in the idea of living day to day. Those landscapes of sand and wind, the cradle of Muslim culture, remind us constantly that man is mistaken when he believes he can leave a trace of himself behind. In the fifteenth century, Ibn Khaldun wrote: 'Arabs spend their entire lives travelling, which is in opposition and contradiction with a fixed life, the producer of civilisation. Stones, for example, serve only as a support for their cooking pots: they take them from buildings, which they destroy to that end. They use wood only to make poles and stakes for their tents.'

Moroccan culture places great importance on destiny, on fortune, on chance events that must be accepted with humility. Unlike what some in the West may believe, this is not always synonymous with resignation or fatalism. There is also great dignity, and a sense of perspective, in this ability to accept one's fate, good or bad. When my father died, I remember those who, when his funeral was over, told me: 'There, he is dead. We have wept and now we must live. Such is God's will.' They repeated to me, like a consolation, this saying, attributed to the Prophet Muhammad: 'Be in this world as if you were a stranger or a traveller along the path. If you survive till late afternoon, do not expect to be alive in the morning.'

For Muslims, life down here is mere vanity, and these popular expressions remind us constantly of this. We are nothing, and we live at the mercy of Allah. The dignity of the believer resides in resignation and his capacity to accept that nothing can last, that all will vanish. Man's presence in this world is ephemeral, and one should not get too attached to it.

A fire is nothing more than a misfortune. A forgotten cigarette, a gust of wind, the absence of rain. People find it hard to accept the cruelty of chance. We revolt against it, we seek meaning in it, a sign, an explanation. Sometimes we imagine that it is a conspiracy or a warning from God. As Kundera writes, 'modern man cheats'. He does not want to look death in the face; he pretends to believe that things will last, that there is a place for eternity. Our societies, which venerate the principle of caution, the idea of zero risk, hate chance because it destroys our dreams of control. Literature, on the other hand, cherishes the scars of accidents, incomprehensible misfortunes, unjust suffering.

I look at my watch. It's barely even midnight. The museum is silent as a cemetery. I could go to bed and when I open my eyes, a few hours from now, it would all be over. I could rediscover the sunlit streets; I could forget my sordid confinement fantasy. I imagine the terrace where I could sit, the cup of espresso I could drink, the cigarette I could smoke.

The cigarette.

I should never have thought about that.

I take a deep breath, hoping there's a trace of nicotine somewhere in my lungs. Who would know if I took a couple of drags? Would the caretaker rush over to stop me? Would I be fined? Thrown out of the museum in the middle of the night? I could just say that I'd forgotten the rule. Or that it was part of the performance. A journalist once remarked of me that I'm 'not very rock 'n' roll', but even so, I could claim it was an act of subversion or nihilism, or say that I'm a hopeless addict.

I go upstairs to grab my bag and then run back downstairs. I enter the cafeteria toilets and lock the cubicle door. In my hands, I hold a cigarette and a toothbrush. This makes me laugh, and I think about those old cartoons where the character is confronted by a choice and two figures appear at his shoulders: an angel and a devil. Two puffs, and no one will know a thing. All I have to do is kneel down, head inside the toilet bowl, then light a cigarette, take a good hard drag and drop it in the water. This is what I do. And instantly start worrying about what will happen if the caretaker wakes up. The smell of smoke fills the toilets. I should run upstairs now and dive under my covers. Pretend to be an innocent asleep.

I've been here for hours now, talking to myself, and I'm starting to feel a bit disoriented. A bit unsure of myself. I feel as if I'm roaming the corridors of a haunted house. I've lost track of where I am, lost track of time. I keep hearing voices. A woman's voice, soft and clear. From here, I can't tell what she's saying. She is speaking English. I lift up a curtain and enter a room plunged into darkness. In front of me is a screen, and now I recognise that voice. It's Marilyn Monroe, with her tell-tale lilt, at once childish and filled with an ageless wisdom. That voice, which mimicked the intonations of beautiful idiots and yet carried all the weight of melancholy. I can hear her speak, but I can't see her face – or that body, which was her glory and her burden.

My parents adored the cinema. When my sisters and I were very young, they used to show us films from the golden age of Hollywood, and their passion for them was obvious. Part of my adolescence played out there, on a sofa squeezed between my two sisters, watching American films. My parents were big fans of Lauren Bacall, Cyd Charisse, Katharine Hepburn. I don't know what they thought of Marilyn Monroe, though I doubt they would have enjoyed seeing their daughters dancing to 'Diamonds Are a Girl's Best Friend'. When she acted in comedies, Marilyn was the precise opposite of what my parents wanted us to be. A fake ingénue, a naive and venal beauty whose only talent was wiggling her hips and getting men to do what she wanted. In *How to Marry a Millionaire*, she refuses to wear glasses because she thinks they make her look ugly, and keeps walking into doors and walls. She was pathetic. I thought her extraordinary.

My sisters and I were fascinated by those films. Never had we seen women like her in real life, as beautiful, as blonde, as stripped bare. Marilyn and the other actresses lived in a distant, unknown world that, film by film, nevertheless became familiar to us. A world where women wore hats and silk gloves, and drank cocktails while sitting alone at bars. A world where women went on cruises with trunks full of clothes, where their dresses were blown upwards in the middle of the street. Where they kissed the men of their dreams in the backs of taxis. I was twelve, with a unibrow and kinky hair. To me, that world seemed far out of reach.

What did I think, the first time I heard women singing that diamonds were their best friends? I don't remember, but I don't think I was shocked. On the contrary, I probably thought it was funny, subversive, delightfully troubling. I wondered what it would feel like to be a woman like that. A woman whose beauty sparked panic on the streets, with hips so curvy, breasts so round and lips so full that they were like an invitation to sex. Marilyn was filmed as an object, gorgeous and provocative. And I thought that it must be terrible, sometimes, to be incapable of invisibility. To be hated by women, desired by men, never taken seriously. After that, I discovered the Marilyn of *The Misfits*, who made me think of Tennessee Williams's heroines:

misunderstood provincial women, flirting with despair and madness. As a teenager, I had dozens of photographs of Marilyn on my bedroom walls. I especially liked the black-and-white pictures taken in New York, in the streets, on the subway, on a balcony. She was made to be seen. I sensed an almost disturbing complicity between Marilyn and the camera, as if she'd been completely absorbed by her own image, as if the lens were a vampire that had sucked her dry. Joyce Carol Oates says all of this in *Blonde*. Above all, she says that we cannot reduce Marilyn to a male fantasy. Marilyn inspires women. And women learn very early to look at the world through a masculine prism. So that is how we see Marilyn, and it's a harrowing sight. There's something monstrous in her. She is a lure, a trap, a rag doll, a quasi-mythological creature invented by shady producers. Marilyn, the ultimate sacrificial victim, was devoured by others. She didn't belong to herself; she was the property of the crowd.

On the screen, I see a pen and words forming on paper. Marilyn, the airhead, the pin-up, wrote a private diary. On the advice of her psychiatrist, Margaret Hohenberg, she bought some notebooks in which to write down her thoughts. Her notes are full of *I should*s and *I ought to*s, orders given to herself, to be a better actress, a calmer person. She spent her life trying to find the words to express the emotions that bubbled up inside her in an incomprehensible hubbub. In *Fragments*, a collection of her poems, notes and letters, we discover that she wrote constantly, on scraps of paper, on napkins, in cookbooks. Friends with Carson McCullers and Truman Capote, married to Arthur Miller, she was a voracious reader. She wanted to learn and was slightly ashamed of her writing, her spelling, her lack of education. On the screen, I see a hotel room. We're in New York, in the suite of the Waldorf Astoria where the actress took refuge under the name of Zelda Zonk. Here, she decided to reinvent herself, to relearn everything, to become a real actress. Slowly, the camera pulls back, and we discover that no human hand is holding that pen. It is a deception, a pretence. A robot is writing and the hotel room is merely a studio film set. The prosody of her voice was reproduced using a computer. Marilyn is there and she is absent. A ghost summoned through the medium of technology. Was she ever anything more than a ghost? Did she really exist?

Philippe Parreno, the artist, is also a demiurge. Just as Berrada inverted night and day, as Roni Horn froze the rippling rush of water, he defies the logic of absence and presence, of fake and genuine, of cinema and real life. He brings the dead back to life. Isn't that what I am trying to do with my novel? When I talked about it to the novelist Claire Messud, she told me that a historical novel was like 'science fiction of the past'. The story we tell never happened, and the past we describe is nothing more than a plausible invention. Writing can give rise to almost supernatural moments when fiction and reality intertwine, when our characters come to life in a way that thrills and frightens us. As if we were drawing on the traces left by the dead to create something living. I once read about an African legend that says the dead continue to live among us for as long as we talk about them. The Senegalese poet and president Léopold Sédar Senghor wrote: 'The dead are not dead.' They do not truly die until the day that the last person to have known them dies. As long as we have something to say about ghosts, as long as memories inhabit us, even silently, even buried in the bottomless abysses of our minds, those ghosts will continue to coexist with the living. On a radio programme yesterday, I heard how, in ancient Rome, one of the worst punishments imposed by the Senate on bankrupt politicians was the *damnatio memoriae*. This ordered all statues of the person to be destroyed, their name to be deleted from all registers, all trace of their existence wiped out forever.

There's no doubt about it: this building is full of ghosts. They've left clues everywhere, like Hansel and Gretel, inviting me to follow their tracks. In a corridor, I observe the sculptures of Tatiana Trouvé. Entitled *Les Gardiens*, these bronze, marble and onyx sculptures reproduce the form of two chairs with cushions moulded by the weight of people. The hollow left behind renders their absence tangible, as if the people who had been sitting there had just stood up and left. In stone, we sense the weight of waiting, of boredom. The illusion is so powerful that I feel sure the absent people are about to return.

I think about him, of course. My father. Everything here brings me back to him. This enclosed space in which I am imprisoned. My solitude. The ghosts of the past. My memories of my father are always the same. We did not contemplate many landscapes together. The years we shared took place in a country without season. Wet winters, sultry summers. A Mediterranean beach, fields of olive trees in a fake Tuscany, and then the big house, where he died, where he suffered with an ennui from which we lacked the ability to distract him. He always sat in the same places – at the table or on the living-room sofa – perhaps because he wanted to help me remember him. The instinct of a patriarch or an old, balding lion, once proud and now mocked. On the sofa, he always sat on the right-hand side. The armrest was blackened by the smoke from his pipes, which he sucked calmly, his mouth barely opened, like a fish at the bottom of an aquarium. My mother chose the sofa fabric. I have no doubt that this took her a long time, that she carefully examined the fabric samples, holding a few of them in front of my father's supremely indifferent face. In the end, she made the decision alone: to upholster the sofa with that burgundy cloth, which had, I think, floral designs on it. Or perhaps some Indian-inspired pattern. Not that it matters. What I remember most of all is that in the place where my father's arm rested, the design had been worn almost invisible. The constant rubbing had frayed the fabric thin in that spot, and a stranger entering our home would probably have imagined that the arm of the sofa was where the cat or dog liked to sit. That the cushions had sunk under the weight of some spoiled, overweight pet. They might have even thought it strange that we should allow an animal to monopolise that central, comfortable spot, from where all the movements of the house and even part of the garden could be observed.

'I am not homesick,' wrote Louise Michel, the French anarchist deported to New Caledonia in the 1870s. 'It is the dead I miss, not my country.' It can take time before we miss the dead. Their absence creates an invisible furrow, and, one day, long after they are gone, you find yourself thinking: 'So it's true – I really did live without them.' I often think that I ought to thank my father for being dead. By passing away, by erasing himself from my life, he opened up paths to me that I would probably never have dared take in his presence. This is a shameful thought, a sad thought, but with the passing of the years, I become ever more aware of its truth. My father was an obstacle. Or, even worse, my very destiny required my father's death.

The little girl in me misses her father. The silent dialogue I carry on with him is filled every day with more anger, rage, helplessness. But I am beginning to think that his death was an act of generosity. That he resolved to die for me, that he left us the way a fire goes out: slowly, painfully. That, by the end, he was nothing more than a hint of blue brightness, wavering and fragile. A voice, a look; two brown, feminine hands that held me back from living. By dying, my father compelled me to avenge him. He forbade me laziness, half-heartedness. He put his hands on my back and pushed me into the void, as do all fathers who fear their children are cowardly or weak.

Pinned to the wall of my office is the letter that the Turkish writer Ahmet Altan wrote to *Le Monde* in September 2017. The journalist was accused of supporting the *coup d'état* on 15 July 2016, and wrote the letter a few days before his trial. I remember the first time I read that letter. My heart ached, and every line brought back the nausea of my adolescence, that bitter taste at the back of my mouth. A taste so familiar to me. Ahmet Altan wrote: 'I am not in prison. I am a writer.' Those words seethed, pounded, exploded inside me at a speed beyond my comprehension. I squeezed my eyes tightly shut. I tried to calm down, but the words continued to follow me like a shadow glimpsed from the corner of my eye, like a mystery waiting to be solved. And then I understood. Or thought I did.

In 2003, my father was incarcerated for a few months in the Salé prison after a trial that had lasted years. As a former bank president, he had been involved in one of the biggest political and financial scandals in Morocco's history. After his release, my father grew ill. He died in 2004. Years later, he was completely exonerated of all charges.

Reading Ahmet Altan's letter, those were the memories that surged back. I thought: *My father is in prison. And I am a writer. He is dead and I am alive.* Through my stories, I try to regain his liberty. I write and I dig a hole in the wall of his cell. I write and every night I file down the bars of a prison. I write and I save him; I give him ways out, new landscapes, characters taking part in extraordinary adventures. I give him a life worthy of him. I give him back the destiny that was stolen from him.

You died to give yourself a second chance, and it seems to me that I am the custodian of that second chance, that it is up to me to write the end of the story. I preserve jasmine in jars, I freeze running water, I resurrect dead actresses that you loved, I sculpt in stone your shape on the sofa.

My father's destiny always weighed on mine. I tried to look away. I wanted to ignore what was staring me in the face. I live in the irrational fear of a curse. I am afraid that the same destiny awaits me: I will raise myself to a great height and I will fall. A slow, dizzying fall. A sad, petty fall, beyond the sight of men, in the shadows of a basement, in the shadow of my silence. I will be hated by the world, and then forgotten. And it seems to me that the more I struggle to avoid this destiny, the more events remind me of its inexorable inevitability. Nothing will allow me to escape it. It is written that this curse will be passed on from father to daughter.

Now I have to tell the story. Of my father's slow descent into hell. His social decline. His incarceration. But none of what I say will be true. Or rather, those who lived through those events will not find in them the cold, objective truth. They will say that I am wrong. They will say I'm making it up. That 'it didn't happen that way'. What I don't know will remain in darkness. I have no wish to solve riddles, fill gaps, re-establish truth or innocence. I have an aversion to explanations. I want to leave the questions unanswered because it is in those gaps, those black holes, that I find the material that suits my soul. It is there that I weave my canvas, that I invent spaces for freedom and for lies – which are, in my eyes, one and the same thing. I advance through dark streets and I create my own landscapes. I invent my crowd, my family. I draw faces.

Many people think that writing is reporting. That talking about yourself is a question of describing what you've seen, faithfully reproducing the reality you have witnessed. I, on the contrary, wish to describe what I have not seen, the things about which I know nothing but that obsess me all the same. To describe those events I didn't witness, but that are nevertheless part of my life. To put words to the silence, to defy amnesia. The purpose of literature is not to restore reality but to fill emptinesses, gaps: not with truth but with fiction. The writer exhumes and, at the same time, creates another reality. It is not a question of invention, but imagination: giving body to a vision, built with scraps of memories and eternal obsessions.

What would my father think of my incarceration fantasy? He would probably make fun of me. 'You want to go to prison instead of me, my girl? You want them to lock you up and throw away the key?' He would look at me, his face lit up by that smile, which was the most beautiful smile in the world. He wouldn't be fooled. He would understand all the despair and perversion that my fantasy contained. He would take me in his arms and console me for my absurd attempts to save him and take his place. Would I ever know what he went through? Is it obscene of me to want to understand what that is like?

What happened to my father was fundamental to my desire to become a writer. I often think of this line from *Emily L.* by Marguerite Duras: 'I have the feeling that once it's in a book it will no longer hurt. That it will cease to be anything. That it will be erased. [. . .] writing is that too, I think: erasing. Replacing.' Or, in a way, correcting. After my father's death, I started writing furiously. I invented worlds where wrongs were righted, where the characters were seen for who they were and were not prisoners of an image that the crowd made of them. I wrote about misunderstood people and I dived deep into their souls, as deep as I could go. I learned to live inside myself, listening closely to my inner voice, to the music and the words that flowed through my mind. I wrote to refuse reality and to save the humiliated. When my father came out of prison, he told me about his inner life. He made me understand that something about him, something inside him, had resisted. That there was in each of us a part that others couldn't reach, couldn't profane. An abyss where freedom was possible. I started to think that this inner life was my salvation, and it was up to me whether it would be lost or kept. From then on, my inner life would be nourished entirely by literature.

In *I Will Never See the World Again*, Ahmet Altan writes:

Yes, I am held in a high-security prison in the middle of a no-man's-land. Yes, I remain inside a cell whose heavy iron door makes a hellish racket whenever it is opened or closed. [. . .] All of this is true but it is not the whole truth. When I awake in winter with the whisper of snow piling up on the other side of the window, I begin the day in that *dacha* with enormous windows where Dr Zhivago once found refuge. Until now, I have never woken up in prison. I am a writer. Wherever you lock me up, I will roam through the limitless world of my mind. Like all writers, I have magic powers. I can pass through walls with ease.

My father was a mysterious man. He didn't talk about himself very often, and I am not trying to solve his mysteries. I carry them around with me, those knotty questions, and it seems to me that they drive me on to follow. But to follow what? To go where? I have no idea. But if prison was fundamental in my writing, it is also because my father and his family – me, my sisters, my mother, all of us – were victims of an injustice. And only literature, to me, appears capable of encompassing such a violent, destructive experience. I often see myself as my characters' defence lawyer. Like someone who is not there to judge them, to lock them up in boxes, but instead to tell their story. To defend the idea that even monsters, even the guilty, have a story. When I write, I am inhabited by the desire to work for the salvation of my characters, to protect their dignity. Literature, in my eyes, is the presumption of innocence. It is even presumption full stop: we presume we are united with the rest of humanity by something in common. We presume that this character, sprung from our imaginations, who has lived through experiences we have never lived through, felt emotions during those experiences that we can understand, even though we have never felt them ourselves. I have always been more than curious about other people. Have always felt a ferocious hunger to know them. A desire to enter inside them, to understand them, to walk in their shoes for a minute, an hour, a lifetime. The fates of others fascinate me, and I feel pain when that fate strikes me as cruel or unjust. I have never been able to relax in the cold comfort of indifference. The passer-by in the street, the baker who talks too loudly, the little old man walking slowly, the nanny daydreaming on a bench . . . they all move me. When we write, we feel an affection for the weaknesses and the faults of others. We understand that we are all alone, but that we are all the same.

What most touches me among the great writers is their consideration. In the books that I love, the authors seem animated by such empathy that even the most insignificant existences, the most ordinary feelings, are clothed in magic. Something great seems to emerge from our miserable lives. Those writers gave me the hope or the illusion that we could understand one another, that we could even forgive or not judge one another. That we were not doomed to cold, endless solitude.

My father read a lot. Books were the fortress in which he locked himself away; he piled them up at his feet like a builder piling up bricks to construct a wall. I recently noticed that in one of the few photographs showing the two of us together, there is a book near him. It's a copy of the French translation of Paul Auster's *Moon Palace*. One day – long after my father had died – I found that copy in my parents' library. I recognised the cover, and I remembered how, as a child, I used to read to impress my father. I thought if I held a book in my hands, he would be interested in me; he would see me. I started reading it. I was halfway through the novel: I'd just reached the part where the character is alone in his apartment, ruined, hopeless, imprisoned within the piles of books that he devours. And then I lost the book on a plane or in a departure lounge. I didn't buy another copy and I never tried to find out what happened at the end of the story.

I don't enjoy thinking about my father. I don't know why. I always feel a certain reticence, a distance. I never dive deeply into those thoughts; I don't let myself surrender to that past. I don't want to. Not once have I wept, alone, saying over and over again how much I miss him. There was something mysterious in him and something unfinished about our relationship. Words left unspoken; experiences unlived. He was part of my family, but he wasn't familiar to me. Perhaps I wanted to conquer him, to understand him, to make him an ally, a friend. He died before I could do any of that. In truth, I don't really like thinking about him, because those thoughts themselves are full of ellipses. I'm incapable of summoning a precise memory, a conversation, a game, a meal. No, there's a gulf in those thoughts, an abyss separating him from me.

Strangely, the more I write about him, the less I feel that he truly existed. My words, instead of giving him life, are transforming him into a character, betraying him. My memory of him is a source of pain. Like scratching at the scabs on my knees when I was a child. It hurt, but I took a sort of odd pleasure in the blood flowing freely again. Writing about him feels the same way. I don't think writers write to gain relief. I don't think my novels will ever overcome the sense of injustice I felt. On the contrary, a writer has an unhealthy attachment to their sufferings, their nightmares. Nothing would be more terrible than being cured of this attachment.

Sometimes I wonder: if I were forced to choose between your survival and writing, what choice would I make? Of course, what I should say is: I would prefer never to have written a word and that you were still here and we hadn't suffered. But I don't know if that's true. Henry de Montherlant was right: 'Writers are monsters.' We're godless, lawless. Vampires.

It is three in the morning and I head towards the belvedere, the pointed tip of the building. I remember that this used to be a customs hall. Authority was exercised here, goods were checked, passes and bans issued. Until the fifteenth century, there was a single customs house for goods arriving by both land and sea, located close to the Arsenal. When that became too small, two zones were created for customs clearance: the Dogana di Terra (Land Customs House) near the Rialto, and the Dogana di Mare (Sea Customs House), which acted as a sort of airlock between the island of Giudecca and the bureaucratic centre of Venice. The current building, which dates from the seventeenth century, was simultaneously entrance and exit, border and passageway, a corridor in which men and objects were subject to examination. Located at the confluence of the two great canals that traverse the city, the Canal Grande and the Canal de la Giudecca, the Sea Customs House was the meeting point of two civilisations: the Germanic-Italian empire and the Arab or Byzantine world. Ships would anchor at the building's pointed tip so that customs officers could board them to inspect the hold and steerage, inventory the cargo, check the accounts books. But the customs house also served as a warehouse. Certain cargo was unloaded, then reloaded on to other ships, making Venice the heart of trade between northern Europe and the Levant. Wine, furs, wood, sugar, oil, spices and silks, imported from the Orient, the Balkans, Egypt and Asia Minor, would pile up in the warehouses before being sold in Italy, France, Flanders or England. Thanks to the Incanto system of auctioning state-owned galleys for commercial purposes, this trading empire had the use of a fleet of thousands of ships that roamed the Mediterranean. Venice was a cosmopolitan city, where Jews, Christians and Moors all came together.

This is what struck me the first time I visited Venice: that it belonged to the East just as much as it did the West. In St Mark's Square, I was reminded of Cairo and Istanbul. The gilding on the façade of the basilica made me think of some Byzantine palace, while the arches resembled the inside of a madrasa or a mosque. In certain alleys, I felt as if I were in the heart of one of those medinas designed by the architects as labyrinths to disorient the invader. I was in Fez or Samarkand. I imagined Moors in turbans getting lost in the *calli* and I remembered that when he created the most famous of them all, Othello, Shakespeare was inspired by a charismatic Moroccan ambassador at the English court. The vegetation was just like that of my childhood: palm trees and orange trees, jasmine climbing up palace walls.

Venice is a city without land. Without soil. Its only resource is salt. All its wealth comes from outside, from beyond, from abroad. I see in this the symbol of my own story. Perhaps this is where I live, in a place that resembles this pointed penin-sula. In a customs house, which is by definition a paradoxical place. I have not completely left my departure point nor fully inhabited my place of arrival. I am in transit. I live between worlds.

So here I am, alone in the heart of the customs house, monarch of this lightless, lifeless, solitary kingdom. I wander from room to room, without having to show my identity papers or give any reason or justification for my movements. I have taken over this territory; I have reversed the usual order of things. I live at night and go to bed at dawn. I do not have to explain myself.

All my life, I've had the impression of being in a minority, of not sharing a common destiny with other people. I have never respected traditions or rites. I am horrified by collective euphoria. In Morocco, I am too Western, too Francophone, too atheist. In France, I can never escape the question of origins: 'In a foreign country in my country itself' (Louis Aragon). For a long time, I hated myself for being so nervous and unstable. My contradictions were unbearable. I wanted people to accept me, and then I didn't want to be one of them. When you have several countries, several cultures, it can lead to a certain confusion. You are from here and also from elsewhere. You always consider yourself a foreigner, but at the same time you hate it when others see you that way. You're a hypocrite. Confronted with a Frenchman who tells me that Muslims are, by their nature, violent misogynists, I will fight tooth and claw to defend the open-mindedness of my Moroccan brethren, providing a thousand examples to prove him wrong. On the other hand, confronted with a Moroccan man who tries to convince me that our country is a gentle, tolerant place, I will argue the exact opposite, emphasising its violence and misogyny.

For a long time, I was preoccupied by the idea of writing without any solid anchorage, unsupported by any foundations. Is it possible to write without a land? What can you write about if you feel like you don't come from anywhere?

In *The Sun Also Rises*, one of Hemingway's characters says: 'You know what's the trouble with you? You're an expatriate. [. . .] Haven't you heard that? Nobody that ever left their own country ever wrote anything worth printing.'

Torn between two communities, writing in an unstable equilibrium, I lacked a territorial matrix. In that regard, Salman Rushdie has an important place in my life. I was eight years old and living in a Muslim country when that man became the subject of a fatwa. He was a traitor, an apostate, the lowest of the low. He had sold his soul to the West; he was an infidel who had renounced the religion of his ancestors to make himself look interesting to white people. Later, I read his books, his interviews, his autobiography, and my admiration for him just kept growing. It was Salman Rushdie who taught me that we are not obliged to write on behalf of our families or our compatriots. That this bastardy, this miscegenation, must be explored to its very end, drunk down to the dregs. Writing isn't the expression of a culture, but the tearing of yourself away from a culture when it closed itself up inside orders and diktats. 'We are like men and women after the fall. We are Hindus who have crossed the black waters; we are Muslims who eat pork. And the result is that we belong partly to the West. Our identity is both plural and partial. Sometimes we feel as if we are astride two cultures, and sometimes as if we are falling between two stools.' To my mind, neither arguments glorifying the richness of miscegenation nor those worrying about its consequences truly grasp the complexity of having a dual identity. It is simultaneously a discomfort and a freedom, a source of sorrow and of exaltation. I was torn between legacies and histories so different that I felt doomed to anxiety. I wanted to join a herd, to feel the joys of belonging, being part of a group, a tribe, a community. I wanted to see the world in black and white, to be free of nuances and doubts. I felt like 'those orchids in tropical forests whose roots, descended from the high branches of acoma crape myrtles, remain suspended between sky and earth. They float, they seek, never knowing the stability of soil.' (Michèle Lacrosil, *Cajou.*)

When I arrived in France, I did not feel entirely foreign. I had the impression that I knew this country, that I understood its codes, its culture, its language. I knew the French, but they didn't know me. Notre-Dame, Flaubert and Truffaut were familiar to me, but they had nothing to say about me; they were completely ignorant of me and yet, by a strange accident of history, they were my heritage.

Maryse Condé, who left her native island of Guadeloupe to study literature in Paris, said in an interview:

> I was not homesick when I arrived in Paris. It was familiar because I'd found what I was looking for: an opening to culture, to philosophy. I was home. French culture was something I possessed, something I had mastered. Something in that society was familiar to me. At the same time, it was in Paris that I became aware of the colour of my skin, that I understood I was Black.

It was in France that I became an Arab. A *beur*. I didn't know what that was. '*Beurs* are Arabs from here,' I was told. Suddenly, arriving in France, I was someone 'of North African origin', from a vague territory without borders, without differences or subtleties. Even worse, I discovered over time that I was, as my friend Olivier Guez so aptly put it, 'the kind of Arab they like'. An Arab who eats pork and drinks alcohol, an unveiled, emancipated woman, more attached than even the French are to ideas of secularism and universality. I was a North African woman with kinky hair and dark skin, with a foreign-sounding name, but I could quote Zola and I had grown up on Hollywood films of the 1950s. I was like them, but with a hint of exoticism, as they liked to tell me.

People don't ask me where I'm from or where I grew up. They ask me what my origins are, and I sometimes reply that, since I'm not a piece of meat or a bottle of wine, I do not have an origin but a nationality, a history, a childhood. Never wholly from here, nor wholly from there, for a long time I felt as if I my identity had been stolen. I felt like a traitor too, since I could never fully embrace the world in which I was living. It was always other people who decided for me what I was.

Since starting work on my current novel, I have read a great deal about the colonial era. Every day, I lose myself in contemplation of that big map of Meknès from 1952. You can clearly see the borders that separate the city's different districts. 'The least possible mixing in the order of cities,' said Hubert Lyautey, the first French Resident-General in Morocco. A logic of segregation prevailed at the time, and my great-grandmother thought it completely normal, even healthy, that Jews, Muslims and Europeans should mingle without living together. Like Berenice Abbott in New York, like Etel Adnan in Beirut, I dream of finding traces of the upheaval of those colonial years on the walls of Meknès. What fingerprints did that era leave on the city and on me? 'The man does not remember the hand that struck him, the darkness that frightened him, as a child,' James Baldwin wrote in *Notes of a Native Son*. 'Nevertheless, the hand and the darkness remain with him, indivisible from himself forever; part of the passion that drives him wherever he thinks to take flight.'

I am the child of a generation with a wounded identity: my parents' generation, who learned about freedom, democracy and women's liberation from the mouths of people who oppressed them in the name of race and colonial ideology. To native peoples, colonial power essentially meant: 'This land is not your land.' It made those natives think: *I live in the country of others. I am a stranger, a fugitive in my own home, in danger, ever-vigilant* – like that anxious young woman walking through the streets of Sarajevo.

I speak that language, the language of the spoils of war, which was taught to my father in a school where he was one of the few Arabs. We spoke French at home, and we lived according to rules that were not always in agreement with the rules outside our house. Like Etel Adnan, I elevated the Arabic language into something mythical; it is a private sorrow, a shame, a lack. I would dream of speaking it with total command and fluency; I wanted to possess all its secrets. When I was a child, we studied Arabic in class, and the teacher devoted a large part of each lesson to teaching us the Quran. She didn't let us ask questions or debate whether something was true. Perhaps it's because of those teaching methods that I failed to master Arabic. One day, the teacher, who was albino and wore shoes so tight that her feet turned blue, announced in a high-pitched voice: 'Those who are not Muslim will not go to Paradise. All unbelievers will end up in the flames of Hell.' I was greatly troubled by this. I remember tears welling in my eyes. I thought about my grandmother, my aunt, all my friends who would be delivered into the clutches of Satan. But I didn't say anything. I didn't dare because I knew that woman's violent reactions; I'd learned that it was safer to remain silent. In the country where I lived, we were taught to bow down before those more fanatical than us; taught not to make a scene, to tread carefully. When conservatism rises, when extremism is woven into the weft of society, you inevitably spend your life lying. Whatever you do, don't say they're not married; never talk about his homosexuality; don't admit that she doesn't observe Ramadan; hide those bottles of alcohol and throw them out at night, a few miles from where you live, wrapped up in plastic bin bags. You are mistrustful of children, who have an annoying habit of telling the truth. My parents would spend hours explaining to me that I had to be careful, discreet. I hated that. I hated my cowardice, my submission to their truth. Rushdie taught me that it is impossible to write without accepting the possibility of betrayal, without revealing truths hidden since childhood.

Colonial oppression, I realised, formed not only minds but bodies too, constraining and imprisoning them. The oppressed person dares not move, rebel, lose her temper, leave her neighbourhood, express herself freely. In *The Wretched of the Earth*, Frantz Fanon writes:

> The first thing that the native learns is to stay in his place, not to move beyond certain limits; that is why the native's dreams are muscular dreams, dreams of action and aggression. I dream that I am jumping, swimming, running, climbing. I dream that I burst out laughing, that I cross the river in a single stride, that I am pursued by cars that never catch me. During

colonialisation, the colonised person is forever freeing himself between nine at night and six in the morning.

So, is that what the night is for? Through the window, I contemplate the palaces, the moored boats. In the distance, I see a purple light flashing. If the night is dangerous, it's because it provides the oppressed with ideas of vengeance, provides prisoners with dreams of escape, beaten women with thoughts of murder. Between nine at night and six in the morning, we dream of reinventing ourselves; we are no longer afraid of betraying anyone or telling the truth; we believe that our actions will have no consequences. We imagine that everything is permitted, that our mistakes will be forgotten, our sins forgiven. Night is the land of reinvention, whispered prayers, erotic passions. Night is the place where utopias have the scent of the possible, where we no longer feel constrained by petty reality. Night is the country of dreams, where we discover that, in the secrecy of our heart, we are host to a multitude of voices and an infinity of worlds. 'I proclaim the Night more truthful than the day,' wrote Senghor in *Ethiopiques*.

I lie down on the camp bed. I close my eyes. I hear the sound of water lapping against the docks. Midway between waking and sleep, I think: *That's what your father would have advised you to do if only you'd listened*. 'Get out! Escape this prison to which you have sent yourself. Prepare to board the world.' Around me, everything is immobile, and I start to hate those silent, inert objects. Those paintings, those screens, those display cases, those hunks of marble, all irritate and worry me.

I have been travelling constantly for the past few months. I've waited in train stations and airports. I've gone through dozens of security checks, crossed borders, handed my passport to police officers of various nationalities. Sometimes I've felt so exhausted, so disoriented, that, waking up in a hotel room, I haven't been able to remember which country I'm in. One morning, in Mexico, there was a knock at my door. I opened it, still half-asleep, and started speaking Arabic to the woman on the other side. The professional trips I have to make as a writer are not adventures or explorations. It is a kind of motionless travel, a series of enclosed spaces, because most of the time I am going straight from a train station to a hotel room, from a hotel room to a conference hall, and then back to a train station. My editor worries about my urge to travel. He wrote to me: 'There's something scary about your frenetic desire to keep moving. It's like the only purpose of your existence now is to get all the pages of your passport stamped and to set foot in every country on earth.' I really don't know what drives me to keep travelling like this all the time. I would like to live in a single place, feel at one with the landscape that surrounds me, savour the natural world and the elements, as described so beautifully by Camus in *Nuptials*, or like Alexis Zorba – the character created by Nikos Kazantzakis in his novel *Zorba the Greek* – who for me represents an inaccessible ideal. This colossus, this lover of food and women, this 'captain of the thousand scars' who fears nothing and no one and whose lust for freedom makes such an impression on the book's narrator. It is the

Aegean Sea that flows through his veins, and his body seems made from the same rock as the mountains of his native land. 'I felt, as I listened to Zorba, that the world was recovering its pristine freshness. All the dulled daily things regained the brightness they had in the beginning, when we came out of the hands of God. Water, women, the stars, bread, returned to their mysterious, primitive origin.'

This might seem paradoxical, but I believe you can only truly live in a place if you have the possibility of leaving it. Living somewhere is the opposite of being imprisoned there, forced to stay. 'If you cannot leave the place where you are, you are on the side of the weak,' writes Fatema Mernissi. In writing this sentence, she was, of course, thinking of women trapped in harems, but also, I feel sure, those young Moroccans who, in the hills of Tangier and on the shores of the Atlantic, dream of going elsewhere and are ready to die to make that dream a reality. Being oppressed, being on the side of the weak, means being restricted to immobility. Not being able to leave your neighbourhood, your social condition, your country.

As a child, I used to see the long queues outside the Spanish, French and Canadian consulates. In the 1990s, the phenomenon of the Harraga grew bigger and bigger. Everyone wanted a visa. Europe became a place that was simultaneously despised and desperately desired. In every city, roof terraces were littered with satellite dishes, those exit doors giving access to an unreachable world, a world seen on television that made its viewers tremble with longing. This is what the Moroccan artist Yto Barrada, who lived and worked in Tangier for many years, called 'the desire for the West'. Since then, I have been obsessed by this fundamental injustice: millions of people are condemned to remain where they are. They are forbidden from travelling, prevented from leaving, imprisoned. This is how our contemporary world is structured: on the basis of unequal access to mobility and location.

My friend, the Moroccan writer Abdellah Taïa, was born in Salé, a working-class city near Rabat, separated from it by the Bou Regreg river. Rabat,

the bourgeois capital, looks down upon the popu-
lace of its twin city, and the border between the
two places is not easily crossed. Abdellah is from a
poor neighbourhood, and when he was eighteen,
he decided – against the advice of many people he
knew – to move to Rabat to study literature.
People tried to dissuade him. They said that a child
from a poor family had no time to lose reading
books in a university. That he should know his
place. Shouldn't get ideas above his station. 'Every
day, I had to take the bus,' he told me once. 'It was
roughly a half-hour trip from my home to the
literature faculty. It was no great distance, and yet
my mother had to make massive sacrifices for me
to be able to travel on that bus. Between 1992 and
1998, she managed to scrape together the twelve
dirhams that I needed every day for the trip.
Without her, without that bus journey, I wouldn't
have been able to free myself from my background,
to escape my fate.' We have often remarked to
each other that if we hadn't both become writers,
if we hadn't both emigrated, we would probably
never have known each other. We would have
lived in two neighbouring cities; perhaps we would

have passed each other in the street or on a beach, but it is highly likely that we would never have become friends. To be free, to be ourselves, we both had to leave the banks of that river. We had to go elsewhere to reinvent ourselves.

'Excuse me, miss, I'm sorry but I have to wake you.'

I feel a hand on my shoulder. I hear a man's voice speaking Italian. I open my eyes. A face leans over mine. I'm so frightened that I fall off my camp bed and bang my head against the floor. The stranger is distraught. He asks me if I'm hurt, if he should call for help. I wave my hands around, I stand up and dust off my dress, pretending that I'm not hurt at all. I have a bump on my forehead, but worse than that, I am deeply embarrassed. I feel sure that this man, acting so considerately towards me, is forcing himself not to laugh so as not to annoy me.

I understand that he is not the caretaker, but that he has to clean this room before the first visitors arrive. It is light outside now, and the night I've just lived through seems utterly unreal. Life

139

goes on, far from my flights of fancy, and this man must start his working day. I push a hand through my dishevelled hair. I signal to him that I am leaving, that I will be quick, that I'm sorry and soon I will be gone, I will be out of his hair. I can't remember where I left my shoes, so I run barefoot through the empty museum. I have the impression that the artworks I conversed with last night have become strangers. They have withdrawn into themselves, and they are blanking me, acting as if we have never met before. I find my ankle boots on the floor near a terrarium. At last, I can smell the night-blooming jasmine. That scent accompanies me as I head towards the door I came in through last night. I push it open, and as I cross the threshold, a question occurs to me: was that door unlocked all night long? Could I, if I'd wanted, have fled the museum in the middle of the night? Could I have escaped?

I have left in such a rush that I don't even know what time it is. The sun is barely up. The city is blue and deserted. Not a sound. No one else on the streets, except a figure running in the distance, which quickly vanishes from sight. I walk past the Salute church; I cross a little wooden bridge. There are no witnesses, so I squeeze my face between the bars of a gate and try to catch a glimpse of the garden inside. Above the wall, I can see palm tree branches and a flowering wisteria, just like in our garden in Rabat. *This house*, I think, *is abandoned*.

In a square, a man is opening up his café. He is putting tables out on the terrace. He watches me. My dress is creased, my hair tangled, and my make-up has run down my cheeks. I have the face of a woman who hasn't slept. What story does it tell? The tale of an unfaithful wife leaving her lover's apartment at dawn? At sixteen, when I first started going out at night, we would sometimes dance until daybreak. We would still be slightly drunk when the first rays of sunlight surprised us. Dawn was at once a relief – I'd survived – and a moment of melancholy. The magic spell was lifted, and I suddenly saw how pale and gaunt my friends looked, their lips twisted with nausea.

The waiter gestures with his chin for me to take a seat. I sit down at a table. I order an espresso and light a cigarette. The square is empty. No one is leaning on the barrier around the fountain. There are no groups of tourists led by a guide holding an umbrella or a flag. Slowly, a ballet begins. Shutters are opened. A woman comes out of an apartment building, carrying her child in her arms. Figures cross the square. By the time my second coffee, strong and hot, is placed on the table, life has already started again.

Soon, I will have to return to my burrow, to sit at my desk once more. I will have to become as immobile, as indifferent to others, as the objects that served as my companions last night. My characters are waiting for me; I must dig them up from the depths, exhume their secrets. I must give life to ghosts. Because literature, like art, pays no attention to the timeframes of everyday life. It doesn't care about the borders between past and present. It makes the future happen now, sends us back to the open woodlands of childhood. The past, when we write, is not dead.

For me, writing has been an act of reparation. A way of making amends for the injustice inflicted upon my father. I wanted to make amends for all the infamies: not only those that affected my family, but also those committed against my people and my gender. I wanted to make amends, too, for my feeling of not belonging to anything, not speaking for anyone, living in a non-place. I might have thought that writing would bring me a stable identity, that it would allow me to invent myself, at least, to define myself beyond the gaze of others. But I have come to understand that this fantasy was an illusion. Being a writer, for me, means being condemned to live on the margins. The more I write, the more excommunicated and foreign I become. I lock myself away for days and nights, trying to express these feelings of shame, unease, loneliness. I live on an island, not to escape other people, but to contemplate them, and, in that way, to satisfy the passion I feel for them. I don't know if writing saved my life. I am generally suspicious of such claims. I would have survived, even if I hadn't been a writer. But I'm not sure I would have been happy.

Acknowledgements

To write is to be alone, but . . .

Many thanks to my editor and friend Alina Gurdiel, without whom this book would not exist. Her enthusiasm and her passion were what made the organisation of that mad night in Venice possible. And she accompanied me through those weeks of writing with a kindness and a gentleness that I still remember fondly. Thank you to Martin Béthenod for welcoming us to the Punta della Dogana and so generously sharing his view of Venice and contemporary art with me. Thank you, too, to Manuel Carcassonne for the sharp, insightful eye he brought to my manuscript and for his passion for literature, which I share. Lastly, I would like to thank my friend Jean-Baptiste Del Amo, who agreed to play the part of my first reader, and whose comments were so helpful to me.